THE TATTERED LITTLE GIRL

KIMBERLEY THOMPSON

BASAR
PUBLISHING

What others are saying........

"In this book, The Tattered Little Girl, Min. Thompson helps you to see that even if your past was traumatic and filled with trauma, God has a plan to deliver you! Freedom comes with a price! Min. Thompson masterfully shares her story to set you on a course that yes, though your past was filled with traumatic experiences, God in His infinite wisdom has a door and a plan to set you free! The door of victory is yours through The Tattered Little Girl!"

-Apostle Christopher Hardy
Presiding Bishop of International Covenant
Life Network

"Sexual Abuse knows no religious, socioeconomic or racial boundaries. Childhood sexual abuse is widespread and is the best kept "dirty little secret" across the nation. If not dealt with, its victims grow into adulthood unable to cope because their heart is trapped in their childhood pain and torment of their past. Raw, powerful and courageously honest, A Tattered Little Girl is the inspiring story of one girl's struggle to become a woman, and her journey exposing the pain and devastation of abuse. Kimberley Thompson doesn't hold back. I respect her honesty and openness as she paves the way as a forerunner sounding the alarm for the multitudes that are still hiding in the darkness, feeling ashamed, tattered and without hope. Her testimony reveals that there is redemption in moving from silence to

healing, from ashes to beauty, from defeat to victory!"

-Kimberly Almeida
Author, *A Mother and Her Prophet, Love's Tapestry*

"It is funny that when the pressures of my past pollute the promise of my present it stunts the possibility of my future if left unchecked by those who have overcome the pain that threatens my eternal purpose. This work removes the mask of silence that demands those wearing the mask to dance around the issues of their existence! The Precious Father will use this work in your life to arrest the shame and suspend our stunted growth. The thing this book will do is literally brings to TOTAL Freedom in the face of your captivity. My prayer is that you read it with all your pain present so that by the end of this literary message you are able to dismiss that which has haunted and kept you bound for years."

-Dr. Jacob Hopson
Founder and Pastor of Destiny Revelation Tabernacle

This riveting life story told by Kim Thompson is a vivid description of how the enemy wants to steal, kill and destroy our lives. She takes you from her past life of devastation to her current life of freedom and victory. I have had the honor of knowing Kim for several years. There are no remaining scars of her traumatic past. What a mighty God! Her life is now a testimony of the power of God. He came to destroy the works of the enemy, give us abundant life and beauty for ashes.

-Dr. Pamela Hardy
Set Free Ministries, Founder of The
Eagles International Training Institute

DEDICATION

The Tattered Little Girl is dedicated to every child who is experiencing the trespass of sexual and emotional abuse, to every teenager who may find themselves in a relationship that strips them of their worth and dignity and to every person who has buried their past and silenced the heart of the little child that lives within. Your breakthrough is now. May the wounded child be healed and set free from the grips of the past. God has given you His beauty for your ashes and for the shame of your youth; He shall give you a double portion.

ACKNOWLEDGEMENTS

To my Lord and Savior, Jesus Christ: Thank You for entrusting me to deliver this word to Your people during this season. You have been my encourager when doubt and fear wanted to silence me. You have given me the strength to tell my story so that others will be blessed. Thank You for Your unfailing love, grace and mercy.

I am blessed to have such a wonderful spiritual family who have stood by me and supported me in all that God has called me to do. Continual blessings to you for you are precious jewels that have been placed in my life: Endtime United Ministries, Apostle and Prophetess Dunlap, Elder and Minister Staley, Elder Melvina Huff, Pastor and Co-Pastor Dudley and Dr. Jacob Hobson. Many blessings to you all.

To my pastor, Elder Joyce Washington, thank you for having the heart of God toward his people. You have always encouraged me to operate in the gifts that God has given me. I truly appreciate your support, love and prayers.

A special thank you to Apostle Chris and Dr. Pamela Hardy for such a vision as Eagles International Training Institute. You have humbly submitted yourselves and allowed the Father to use you to birth gifts out of his people. Without you, this ministry of writing may not have come to pass. I am forever grateful for your prayers, encouragement, teachings and covering.

Thank you Pastor Rekesha Pittman for walking me through this awesome journey that released me to "GET WRITE!"

To Candace Ford, Love Clone Publishing, thank you for your editorial and publishing support. You have been a tremendous blessing.

To Kimberly Almeida, my spiritual Jonathan. We have been through so much and yet God has preserved us to see a season that will propel us both deeper into His will for our lives. Thank you for loving me, supporting me and understanding me when I sometimes did not understand myself. What a priceless gift you are. Love you, my sister.

And I have saved the best for last. Thank you Bill and Cyrilla Thompson for parenting me. Words cannot express the gratitude that I have that God choose you just for me. Thank you for encouraging me to always be the best that I can be and for teaching me about integrity and strength. I love you both more than you know.

CONTENTS

FOREWORD

It is a great pleasure for me to recommend and introduce author, Kimberley Thompson's newest book, The Tattered Little Girl.

I have known Kimberley since 1988. In that time, I have found her to be a woman of integrity, full of tender mercies and compassion. She has a strong faith in God that shows in her walk of life. Kimberley has been greatly used of the Lord in many facets. Her life has been transformed out of the cocoon into a beautiful butterfly.

Kimberley offers to you a glimpse into the windows of her past and present. She shares the reality and experiences of "the tattered little girl" as they happened. Yet she will show you how she emerged from victim to victor.

I thoroughly enjoyed reading this book. It took me back into my own experience of abuse and how it is possible for God to take such trauma and use it for his glory. As you begin to read through the pages of this book, you will discover how important it is to raise a child in a well-nourished environment. That makes up the blueprint through their adult life.

Young children that suffer sexual abuse, emotional abuse and physical abuse are unaware how these "spiritual doors" will affect them. Mostly, through their adult life many wear masks to masquerade the pain and the shame they encountered. Outside you cannot see the trauma, her life, her pain, the scars but inside the wounds are still fresh as though the incident has just occurred.

Readers, you will be swept away into her life her pain, her triumph. Every chapter will unpeel layer after layer bringing about wholeness, healing and victory. It will be a beginning of a new you. Kimberley, through her story wants you to know it is possible to come out from under the ashes of despair and hopelessness and arise a beautiful soul fit for the Master's use.

You will never be the same again...

Prophetess Paula Dunlap, Associate Pastor
St. Paul Deliverance Christian Center

INTRODUCTION

A Broken Beginning

I have always been a master at masking my true emotions. I perfected this talent for inventing different characters at a very young age to hide who I really was. My childhood and young adult life appeared to be one big masquerade. This emotional facade served me well as a child and became a smokescreen to my true identity in my adulthood, thus hiding the person that I was really called to be.

As a young girl I acquired several emotional masks that became very much a part of me and my everyday existence. I adorned them regularly and became quite comfortable at being what everyone needed me to be but not being who I really was and not quite knowing who I was. When I wore my masks no one knew what I was thinking, there was no insight given as to what I was feeling and more importantly no one had any inkling of what I was hiding. No one knew of the hidden childhood experiences that had birthed emotional setbacks in my life.

I came to love and heavily depend on my masks because they allowed me to become someone that I yearned to be and leave behind the one that I loathed. These well placed cover ups gave me permission to smile when I was hurting, to laugh when I wanted to cry, to appear beautiful when I saw myself as ugly, to love myself when I secretly detested my very existence, to be strong when weakness was overtaking me and to live when I wanted to curl up in a ball and die. This charade allowed me to hide all of my "dirty little secrets" and be everything to everyone and nothing to myself.

To look at me, to talk with me or even to spend time with me, no one would think that I did not have it all together. No one would have ever known the turmoil and anguish my soul was suffering. Feelings of abandonment, insecurity and self-loathing were undetectable to someone looking on but were very much alive in me and were a part of my daily conflict. My masquerade buried my inner thoughts and struggles and silenced the screams of a tormented and broken child. The child within was suffering from past emotional wounds that birthed the feelings of rejection, abandonment, insecurity and self-loathing. That child had become a victim of someone's warped affections that drew her into an illegal sexual relationship with an uncle. It was a relationship that left deep emotional scars on the soul of a child. These unhealed scars became a burden that carried over into adulthood.

For the majority of my life I had been perpetrating a fraud and no one was the wiser. I had become an emotional chameleon capable of conforming to what I needed to be for emotional survival but in reality I was dying inside.

This is what victims of child abuse do. They suffer in silence as they hide behind the masks that lead you to believe that all is well, when truthfully they are torn apart emotionally and mentally. Any form of abuse

Actual cutting.

inflicted upon a child is a horrific crime. It is the sort of crime that releases heaviness upon a heart and leaves that heart to grieve and mourn the plight of the child. It is the type of crime that unleashes an unquenchable rage toward the perpetrator. This is a wrongdoing that no child should ever have to endure, but unfortunately in our fallen world, abuse of all forms is rampant and claiming the lives of our children.

Childhood sexual abuse is one of the most painful, degrading, and hidden secrets that can be kept by victims who are too young and emotionally immature to own it. This form of abuse is designed to strip the victim of their innocence, rob them of their self-worth, and give them a false identity.

Sexual abuse takes many forms and occurs through rape, incest, fondling, introducing one's prey to pornography or exposing oneself to someone. It is the act of a predator upon the innocent for self-gratification. This form of abuse and its effects can be compared to the actions of a boa constrictor when it conquers its prey. A boa constrictor catches its prey with its powerful jaws. Once the jaws of the constrictor are locked on its prey, the constrictor coils its body around the prey and squeezes until there is no more evidence of life. The more the victim struggles to get free the tighter the grip becomes. Like the jaws of the constrictor that subdues his prey, the sexual trespass grips and subdues the victim. Once this trespass has gotten a tight grip around the victim's soul, shame, condemnation, and the feeling of worthlessness wraps itself around the mind and emotions of its victim and suffocates the very life out of them. It causes them to live with shame and condemnation as a child and well into their adulthood. Like the prey that is wrapped in the coils of the constrictor, the abused victim is wrapped in the coils of despair. This despair may manifest in a child through violent acts or acts of rebellion. He or she may become withdrawn or unsociable and may have a difficult time communicating. Adults who have not been healed from childhood abuse may try to escape the reality of their pain through means of alcohol, drugs, promiscuity or denial. Unfortunately for both adult and child, their meager attempts to be set free of the pain only cause the grip of despair to tighten its coils around their soul and drain them emotionally and mentally until no evidence of life remains.

The feelings of shame and guilt often place the victim in a "hush, don't tell" state of mind. This state of mind is designed to instill fear of what others will think and causes them to take on the blame for the incident. Instead of speaking out, the child buries the abuse deep within with little to no hope of being released from the masquerade of their torn childhood.

"For we wrestle not against flesh and blood, but against principalities, against powers, against rulers of the darkness of this world, against spiritual wickedness in high places." (Ephesians 6:12 KJV)

It is imperative that we understand that we live in a spiritual as well as a natural world and just as things take place in the natural realm, things are taking place in the spiritual realm. Our Adversary, Satan, is an unseen enemy and we are constantly engaged in spiritual warfare. His agenda is to disrupt and possess the soul of man.

The Adversary is very cunning and he does not fight fair. The earlier he can obtain legal rights to you by disrupting your emotional well-being, the greater the chance he has of defeating you. He targets the young and innocent because they are physically, mentally, emotionally and spiritually incapable of defending themselves. His attacks are fruitful at this vulnerable stage because it is a critical time of mental and emotional development for a child. If the Adversary is successful in arresting any part of the child's emotional and mental development, spiritual doors are opened and legal access is granted.

A spiritual door is an opening that Satan uses to access our soul. The soul is comprised of mind, emotions and will. Once spiritual doors are opened, strongholds, which are areas where an enemy dominates, are released in a child's life. The purpose of these strongholds is to dominate the thought process and the emotional stability of the child. These spiritual doors are often opened through some sort of trauma such as emotional, physical or sexual abuse.

Satan uses this strategy because he is aware of the plans and purposes that God has for our lives and he will use any means necessary to disrupt those plans.

He knows that we are predestined from the beginning of time and at the appropriate time we will respond to God's call. We are equipped to be an affective threat against his kingdom and this is something that he cannot allow. If he can disrupt our emotional well-being and fragment our soul at an early age, he has the means to cause us to lead a dysfunctional and perverted life as adults.

Webster defines perversion as a sexual practice or an act considered deviant. A deviant is one whose behavior and attitudes differ from the norm or from accepted moral and social standards. I choose to define these words because when you begin to examine the behavior of one that has been abused, it can fall into the category of that of a deviant. Their perspective, reasoning and behavior will often differ from that of the norm.

When children suffer any type of emotional, physical, or sexual abuse, the door is opened to that perverse spirit and legal access is gained to their mind and emotions, which will affect the will of the one abused. This spirit does exactly what it is defined as, it causes a deviation from moral and social standards. It has the ability to twist the truth and causes the victim to believe that right is wrong and wrong is right. Its purpose is to distort our perspective of our self-worth and cause us to embrace the lie that we are worthless and accept what will hurt us and despise what will love us. Our true identity of who God says who we are is stolen and we go through life aimlessly without any indication of who we really are and what our purpose is.

Looking back to my childhood, I can clearly see how the devil set me up for destruction with the weapon of abuse. By any means necessary, he was going to prevent me from being what God had intended and ordained me to be. He used those closest to me to plant seeds of perversion that gave me a warped perspective of what true love entailed. I suffered from wounds afflicted upon my mind and emotions from those that I loved and who were supposed to have loved me. For many years I battled with the stigma of my past and the pain of my youth. I walked about not knowing who I was because I had accepted the lie that I was nothing. Shame and condemnation stood as judge and jury and I was sentenced to a life deprived of joy, forgiveness and emotional freedom.

But today I rise and stand to say that through repentance, forgiveness and the healing power of Jesus Christ, I have risen from the ashes and the shame of my youth to restored identity, unspeakable joy and a life that has embraced deliverance and victory. This is my story.

CHAPTER 1

Planted Seeds

I was born to Bill and Geraldine Thompson on May 15, 1968 in Chicago, Illinois. My parents were young and from what I've been told, they were very much in love. I've seen photos of them together and those photographs displayed a man and a woman who appeared to be very much in love but as a child, I was not fortunate enough to experience the love that they had for one another. They had separated and divorced before I was old enough to fully understand and appreciate a nuclear family structure.

Bill Thompson was a man's man, full of wisdom and street smarts. He was the product of a broken home, yet he did not allow his troubled upbringing to prevent him from striving to be better than the poor examples he had in his childhood. Bill was the oldest of three boys and I imagine they looked up to him for everything, including filling in for the father figure that they all lacked.

While growing up, my dad did not have a solid relationship with his own father, and this undoubtedly left him with unresolved feelings of abandonment and rejection. The absence of his father did not hinder his desire or his ability to be a good father himself, but it did leave him emotionally crippled. He was raised primarily by his mother Lular and her sister, Thammar, who were both old school, Apostolic, churchgoing women. My grandmother, Lular, was a sickly woman, which caused my father and my two uncles, Gregory and David, to move back and forth from her house to Aunt Thammar's house. Aunt Thammar was a very stern Christian woman with little to no tolerance for worldly pleasure, so you can imagine the restriction that three young boys must have felt and the rebellion that was birthed from it.

Growing up, my father spent a lot of time in juvenile detention like many other African American males raised in the inner city of Chicago. Without the consistent presence of a father, his primary upbringing and teachings came from the streets. This type of upbringing hardens one and can lead to an inability to openly express love.

I am sure growing up without a father was difficult for my father. My grandfather was not in his life on a consistent basis and when he was around, he was a poor example. What my father could have taken from his father was how to mistreat women, for he had experienced that by looking at how my grandfather treated my grandmother. In essence, my father had no one to tell him who he was and no one to really show him how to be a man. My grandfather did not take the proper position in my father's life by imparting those things that would aid him in becoming the man that he was purposed by God to be. My grandfather fell far short of the mark in that aspect. This left my father to take his pointers and gain wisdom from the men on the street.

My father was short in stature but by no means was he a punk. Street life has a way of teaching one how to survive and no doubt the experience that he gained from the street and the time spent in juvenile detention taught him that weakness was not an option. Instead, he learned the value of being strong and the value of knowing how to fight.

The absence of a strong male figure hindered my father's emotional growth and made it very hard for him to openly express love outside of being a provider. In many ways my father was emotionally broken but the love that he had for his children could never be questioned. He wasn't one who had children with different women and believed in taking care of what belonged to him. There was never a time that I doubted my father's love for me and he affectionately called me his "million dollars." He had a heart for children and when he married Geraldine, his heart allowed him to raise my sister, Tonya, who was not biologically his child, as his very own. It takes a strong man with a heart of love to raise another man's child. His favorite motto was "Children did not ask to come into this world so it is our responsibility as parents to make sure that they are okay and taken care of." I admire my father for stepping up and being the man that he was supposed to be in my life. As a daughter, my father was the first male teacher that I had. I gained my strength and independence from him.

My mother, Geraldine, on the other hand, is somewhat of a mystery to me. I did not have the opportunity to grow up with her and get to know her. My childhood memories are very vague and they cannot support any real relationship that we may have shared. From what I have been told, she was a very bright young lady who loved to read for hours. Geraldine was a petite, dark-skinned beauty with eyes that would captivate you and a smile that would light up her face and draw you in. Her sense of style earned many a second glance as she walked down the street. I am blessed to have inherited her eyes, her smile and her lovely chocolate skin. She was raised in a two-parent home and from what I have discovered later on in life, she was dearly loved by her father but maybe not so much by her mother, for she endured many beatings at the hands of her mother.

As an adult, she suffered from what we would diagnose today as bipolar disorder and depression with symptoms of schizophrenia. She, like my father, suffered emotional brokenness as a child and was emotionally fragmented as an adult. Parents are the first teachers that impart to their children and are capable of giving only what they know to give. If they did not grow up in a home that expressed physical love through hugs, kisses and general affection, then it may be hard for them to impart that into their children. I know now that Geraldine loved me, but I strongly believe that she was incapable of imparting into me the emotional foundation that a child ideally receives from their mother, but she could not give what she did not have.

My parents were very young when they married and because of the emotional instability they both had experienced growing up, neither one was emotionally

THE TATTERED LITTLE GIRL

equipped to sustain the other. During their marriage, Geraldine unfortunately fell victim to heroin addiction and became a somewhat functioning drug addict. Her addiction coupled with being bipolar, opened the spiritual door for paranoia to captivate her mind. Undoubtedly paranoia put her in a state of mind that someone was constantly out to get her because she always carried a knife for protection.

Geraldine's drug addiction caused great conflict in her and my father's marriage. The event that ended their marriage was an argument turned violent. They were arguing as they came through the front door one day. My sister, who was in the nearby room, could hear the yelling. I was a baby and my sister was about two or three years old. We lived in the projects then so there was only one door in and one door out. My father came in, bolted the front door and threw something on the table while yelling, "You want to get high? We are going to get high all night." His anger toward Geraldine was due to his frustration with her drug use and he demanded that she stop. They argued for quite some time and as they walked into their bedroom the argument escalated into a physical confrontation. My father cornered Geraldine and threatened to bash her head in with a hammer. He slapped her and began to walk away. As my father was walking away, Geraldine, out of her anger or fear, lashed out and stabbed him at the base of the right side of his neck. I can almost see the shock on his face as he whirled around while placing his hand on his wound. He stumbled to the bedroom door and into the hallway using the wall as support. He got to the front door and attempted to open the locks that he had bolted earlier. Before he could escape, Geraldine lunged at him and began to strike with her knife and stabbed him thirteen times. Between her stabbing him and him trying to get away, he somehow managed to strike her in the back of her head with the hammer he had threatened her with earlier. He finally managed to get outside of the door and staggered down the hallway. Neighbors no doubt heard the commotion and came out of their apartments to see what was going on. One of the neighbors found my father in the hallway bloody and fighting for his life and called an ambulance and the police.

As my sister emerged from the bedroom, she saw the results of an altercation that almost ended in death. Blood saturated the hallway walls and it was very evident that something very traumatic had taken place. The spirit of murder was no doubt lingering in the midst. My father was rushed to the hospital and it was only by the grace of God that he lived and suffered no permanent muscle damage. Geraldine was placed under arrest and spent a week in jail. I believe charges were dropped and she did not serve any jail time for the stabbing. My sister and I were picked up by Geraldine's parents, Ma and Pop Dunigan and taken to their house.

Although my father believed in family, he knew that he could not be a part of this family any longer. He could not go back after what had occurred. He was fed up with all the drugs and all the drama that went along with it and more importantly, he almost lost his life and could have taken Geraldine's life. I can only imagine the pain he must have felt as he lay in his hospital bed cut, bruised, and bandaged, as the harsh reality of losing his family became more and more evident. How he must have wrestled with his heart and emotions with the decision he had to make in order to secure safety not only for himself but for his child.

As he lay in his hospital bed, Bill told Geraldine's parents, Pop and Ma Dunigan, and my sister, Tonya that when he got out of the hospital he was leaving Geraldine and he would be taking me with him and they would never see me again. At that moment, he did not realize that his decision would not only affect the life of his daughter, me, but would be a major impact on the life of my sister as well, for he was the only father that she knew.

My early childhood years are somewhat vague to me. There are certain things that I remember clearly and some things that are cloudy flashbacks or scattered pieces of a puzzle. I remember times with Geraldine and my sister but it is not a consistent flow of memory. I know I loved my sister dearly. I looked up to her and followed her around as only a little sister would. I loved her and wanted to be in everything that she was in. I was always protective of her and in one incident, while we were at the corner store, I took on a boy twice my age and size when I thought he posed a threat to her. I only saw Tonya when I visited Geraldine and in the end it was not frequent.

As I grew older, and my father remarried, I lost contact with her altogether. It's funny, as an adult I would think of her quite often and would dream of her a lot. It was sad because in those dreams I would never see her face. I had no idea what she looked like and I would often say I wouldn't recognize her if I passed her on the street. I would find myself praying for her well-being and asking God to one day bring us back together. God is a prayer answering God and after 30 plus years He did just that. We were reconnected. Tonya lives in Georgia and is doing well. We are rebuilding a relationship that was lost.

Although my parents had separated, I still spent a lot of time with Geraldine. My father worked diligently to get a divorce and full custody but for the most part I was still with Geraldine. When you think of a mother and daughter relationship you may instantly think of a special bond between a mother and her child. A mother is the first teacher that a daughter has and it is imperative that the bond between mother and child be established immediately after birth. A daughter needs her mother to teach her everything that she needs to know about being a woman. When that teaching does not come from her or is distorted, the daughter suffers and becomes in danger of leading a dysfunctional life, often following in the destructive patterns of the mother. A mother has spiritual authority in her child's life and can impart life or death. Theirs is a bond that forever connects them one to another. In the end, a mother is the best gift that a daughter could ever have or the worst enemy a girl can encounter.

My relationship with Geraldine was not the ideal I just described. There was never a special bond that we shared and for a long time, even until recently, I thought that she did not love me at all. She did not raise me for long, so what I do remember of her and our time together is like clips that you would see in a movie, one scene and then the next pasted together in a simulation of reality. Geraldine's parenting skills were undoubtedly questionable. For example, when my father came to pick me up and found me in a diaper that I had been in for two days. The horror he must have felt as he rushed his child, me, who had sat in a soiled diaper for two days, to the emergency room to have the diaper removed and me treated for possible sever diaper rash and ammonia burns.

Even though there were incidents such as that, I stayed with my mom and sister for quite some time after my parents separated. We lived in a three-bedroom apartment. The bedroom I shared with my sister was off of the living room. There was a bedroom down the hall to the right and Geraldine's bedroom was located in the back off of the kitchen. During the time that I was with her, I never witnessed her using drugs so whether she was still using drugs or not, while I was in her custody, I am not sure. However, I do know, from her behavior, depression got the best of her. This was evident when she took the liberty of painting our dining room walls black. I will never forget standing in the entrance of the dining room and watching her fervently paint the walls. As I stood there and watched her paint, it was as if something was controlling her. I can't imagine what she must have been thinking but it was as if she was trying to block out anything that would offer light and life. Depression had engulfed her and it was a ruling factor. The black paint on the dining room walls was a clear depiction of the blackness that engulfed her life.

Her distance toward me caused me to feel rejected and detached from her. I can't remember a time when I heard Geraldine tell me that she loved me nor can I recall her ever embracing me. I am not saying that she didn't, I just don't have any memory of her doing so. I do recall her getting so angry with me for biting my sister that she viciously grabbed me while yelling and bit me so hard on my left arm that it left teeth marks. I ran into my bedroom holding my arm while screaming at the top of my lungs. It felt as if my arm was going to fall off as the dull ache of pain coursed through my body. If I allow myself to think about it, I can still feel the anger in her grip and the sting of her teeth tearing into my flesh.

Since Geraldine and my father were no longer together I was exposed to some of the men that she dated. The men in her life were never kind to her; in fact, some could be downright cruel. Because of her emotional brokenness, she attracted abusers and losers. I distinctly recall a time when I stood and watched her boyfriend punch her in the face. He punched her in her face as if he was punching a man and left her crumpled on the floor at the foot of the bed to think about why she had gotten hit. As she lay in the bed crying, I slowly walked to the bathroom for a cool towel to place on her swollen face. As I placed that towel on her inflamed cheek and gazed into her beautiful, blackened dark eyes - eyes that revealed her broken life - I had no concept of the spiritual transference that was taking place. What a sight for a young child to witness her mother, whom she loved so much, beaten and broken at the hands of an abuser. My mind was whirling. Was this how a man and a woman interacted? Was this type of abuse acceptable? Is this love? Why was my mommy, the woman who gave me life and who was supposed to groom me into a strong, virtuous woman, lying in bed shattered and beaten? She had nothing to offer; she had nothing to give.

I went back into the living room and looked that joker right in his face, a face that showed no remorse. As I sat on the floor, I looked between him and the television and the emotional rage that I felt was too much for a young soul to bear. I wanted to strike out against him for what he did. I wanted to protect my mother from this beast of a man. At one point, I looked him directly in his eyes and he turned his face and dropped his head.

From the age of four up until seven I lived with my grandma Lular, my father's mother, because of my parent's break up. I was too young to understand the reason for the break up; all I remember was that my

father and my uncle Gregory came to Geraldine's
apartment one night. Geraldine hid me and would
not let them in. My father later came back with the
police and carried me out crying and screaming to
stay with Geraldine. We went to my grandmother's
house and he placed his crying child on the couch
while he explained to his mother what had happened.
I sat there crying with my thumb in my mouth trying
to self soothe. In spite of all that Geraldine did and
didn't do for me, I still loved her and the thought of
being away from her was unbearable and quite
traumatizing. It is amazing how one can cling to
something or someone that is not emotionally good
for them. Although Geraldine was my mother,
emotionally she was not good for me. In her current
drug addicted state, she was incapable of being any
type of mother, much less a good one, but in spite of
all of that, she was all that I knew and I wanted to be
in that familiar place. As I calmed down and slowly
began to rock myself, a strange realization came over
me. At four years old, I knew that I was not going
back. Grandma Lular became my caretaker and her
home my permanent residence with periodic visits to
see my mom and my sister.

I don't fault Geraldine because she was wrestling
with demons unaware. I have come to find out that
even in her broken state she loved me more than I
could have imagined and that there are always two
sides to every story and then there is God's truth of
what really took place. I can say that in the end, the
Lord was faithful and he saved Geraldine, delivered

her from drugs and the sting of abuse and took her home in 1986. I rejoice in her healing.

My grandmother Lular was a God-fearing woman who loved the Lord deeply. I know this because I remember trips to the storefront church, testimony and an occasional foot washing service. She was short in stature with a chocolate brown complexion and wore glasses. Grandma Lular was on the sickly side and had dealt with TB as a young adult. Later cancer, which took one of her breast. Her right arm was twice the size of the left and she suffered from coughing spells that often resulted in her spitting up phlegm and blood.

I was my grandmother's first grandchild. She was the mother of three boys, my father Bill, and my two uncles, David and Gregory. I was the girl that she never had and she loved me dearly. I loved her even more.

She lived in a quaint little yellow house on the south side of Chicago. It was a three-bedroom house that had a living room, dining room, kitchen and basement. There was always love in her house. During the time that I lived there, several relatives would stay with us. I had a lot of cousins and on occasion the back bedroom or the basement would be occupied with someone that needed a temporary place to stay. At one point in time, my uncle Gregory, his wife and two sons stayed with us. My grandmother had a soft heart and would rarely turn anyone down who she thought was in need.

Even though she was saved and loved the Lord, as I look back and begin to analyze some things from a spiritual point of view, she did not recognize some of the spiritual doors that were open in her home. My uncle David was a victim of an open spiritual door. I can remember him always being a nice and gentle man who was full of life. Something happened that resulted in him losing his senses. One of my memories of him was of him in the living room, sitting in a chair in the corner literally foaming at the mouth as he stared into space. I sat there in front of him and just stared at him and when I attempted to wipe the spit from his chin he abruptly pushed my hand away. In thinking back, I was sitting at the feet of a man who was under the influence of an evil spirit. I know now that God had his hand on my life and had protected me that day.

"The thief cometh not, but for to steal, and to kill, and to destroy." (John 10:10 KJV)

Satan comes to steal our identity, kill us spiritually and destroy our purpose. I was an easy target for Satan because of the emotional trauma and soul wounds I had endured very early on in my childhood. He used my parents' emotional brokenness to plant seeds of dysfunction when it came to relationships and love. The harshness of my parents' break up and the separation from my mother left me emotionally shattered and struggling with abandonment and rejection issues. The abusive men in Geraldine's life left me with a distorted view of what love should be between a man and a woman. But the enemy did not stop at emotional distress. His aim was to completely arrest my emotional development so that I would lead a defective life. The seeds of emotional dysfunction had already been planted. Now his aim was to plant seeds of sexual lust that would ultimately birth the stronghold of perversion.

There are several incidents that took place that the enemy used to plant the seed of sexual perversion. One incident was through the actions of my mother, Geraldine, and his opening was my eye gate. This occurrence happened while I was still in her care. I was at home but I'm not sure where my sister was at the time. I went into the back of the apartment looking for her. Her bedroom was off and to the right of the kitchen. Her door was not closed and I walked up to the doorway of her room just in time to catch her in bed with a short middle-aged bald white man and another woman. To this day I can remember standing at the door and seeing this man, along with my mother and the other woman, jump up in surprise. I'll never forget that image as I stood there in the doorway trying to wrap my child's mind around what was going on. The man was wearing a white t-shirt, a pair of boxers and socks and the women scrambled about trying to hide their nakedness. I stood there not quite grasping what I was looking at but knowing that I was getting yelled at for something that they deemed I did wrong. This incident released the seed of lesbianism and lasciviousness.

The enemy also used my mother's brother to impart sexual seeds through my ear gate as I lay in bed with my sister and listened to him have sex with his girlfriend in the next bed. Although I was too young to intellectually comprehend what was actually taking place, my spirit was receiving what was taking place.

Although these two incidents, I believe, played a major part in opening the door to the enemy, there is one occurrence where that perverse spirit appeared to me through a dream type vision. I remember it as vividly today as I did when it first happened. I was about five years old and I was living with my grandmother Lular. My bedroom was my grandmother's living room couch. It was a yellow couch that had the classic plastic covering on it. It was the love seat of the living room combo and it was located on the left side wall as you walked into the living room. Across from the love seat was the full sized couch where my grandmother was sleeping that night. Between the two couches was the coffee table. I was up that night trying to rock myself to sleep. Rocking and sucking my thumb was what I did to soothe myself. I was up that night while everyone else was asleep. I recall sitting up and looking across the room at my grandmother lying on the couch asleep. As I looked at her, something moved and caught my eye. I looked toward the window and saw a shadow of a black male figure and the shadow of a black female figure. These figures had no faces but their bodies were fully formed. He was very masculine and the female was full figured. They resembled the characters from a "black love" poster but were faceless. I specifically remember them being covered in honey and nuts (strange, I know). I was fixated at what I was seeing but oddly enough I was not afraid.

While looking at these figures, the woman kneeled on the coffee table on her hands and knees, taking on a doggie style position. The man came behind her and penetrated her, but as he penetrated her, I physically felt the penetration. I can recall the stickiness and coarseness of his penis as it entered me. I didn't scream, I didn't call for my grandmother; strangely enough I just sat there. What was happening to me was so surreal. I had no idea at that time that I was being raped in the spirit. As I ponder that incident today, I believe that the spirits Incubus and Secubus, male and female sexual demons that visit in the night, were present in that room that night.

Needless to say, psychologically, I was not quite the same after that experience. I was young and had no comprehension of what took place that night. As far as I was concerned it was a crazy dream. I had no idea of who or even how to tell what took place so I repressed it by forgetting about it. I went on with my days as I always did but there was a change. The spirit of seduction was heavy on me and I became a little bit more aware of boys than an average five to six-year old should be. There was also an encounter with a certain little boy that went beyond the scope of "you show me yours and I'll show you mine." It was my first experience with oral sex.

My first grade best friend and I shared moments that slightly opened the spiritual door to lesbianism. That seed had already been planted when I witnessed Geraldine in bed with the man and the woman. I was engaging in sexual curiosities without having the knowledge of what it was. I did know that it stimulated me and physically it felt good. I realize now that a sexual spirit had been assigned to me to pervert my life early on.

Anger also became a big factor. I was always mad and my anger was volatile. It manifested itself through physical attacks on other children and temper tantrums. I remember standing in line to be dismissed from school and for some reason I attacked the little boy in front of me. I viciously stabbed him in his face with a pencil just a fraction from his right eye, then violently pushed him against the desk and watched him fall. I don't know why I did it, and I don't believe he provoked me in any way that would cause me to retaliate. I do know his mother was angry and she dragged me kicking and screaming to the principal's office and even then I was pulling away from her and trying to control the situation. My anger manifested in a subtle way when I took a razor blade and cut up my cousin's hand. I wasn't mad at my cousin; I just wanted to see what would happen if I ran the blade across his hand. He was bleeding profusely as they wrapped his hand in a towel and carried him to the hospital. I had never seen my aunt cry like I saw her cry that day. As if that was not enough, another display of how anger had a grip on me was my revenge on a boarder who was residing at my grandmother's house.

Ms. William was an elderly lady living with us. She was an amputee and was confined to a wheelchair. We never really got along and I don't know what took place that resulted in her kicking me but my revenge on her for kicking me was greater. I poured Lysol in her glass of water and encouraged her to drink it hoping that it would make her sick. She drank it just so I would stop asking her to drink it and she immediately spit it out and called for my grandmother yelling that I was trying to kill her. As my father walked through the door that night, the look on his face was that of anger. My grandmother had called him and told him what I had done. He had gotten out of bed to drive all the way over to the other side of town to discipline me. That night I received the whipping of my life from my father but even with that, I felt no real remorse for what I had done.

I was an unruly child with a lot of deep seated issues that manifested themselves through anger. Because I was a child, I was not aware of and definitely not equipped emotionally to process the passions that I was dealing with, so my release came through outbursts of violence.

These early childhood events made me an easy target for Satan. I say "easy" target because my soul was already in a place that needed repair and seeds of dysfunction had been planted through the actions of those that were responsible for nurturing and protecting me. I had been set up very early on to respond to abuse.

CHAPTER 2

The Transition

At the age of seven my life changed. That change began with my father marrying my mother, Cyrilla Perez and me leaving my grandmother's home to live with them. My father had dated Cyrilla for quite some time so we had already established a good relationship. I remember the first time I met her, I liked her instantly. The first time my father left me alone with her for a day, when he came back to pick me up, he was astonished that I was calling her mom. He thought that she had put me up to it but that was not the case at all. I liked her from the moment I saw her and that day we spent coloring and eating popcorn gave me the motherly love and attention that I had been missing. Trust and a sense of security had developed between a potential mother and a needy child. In looking back, I truly believe that God orchestrated the union between Cyrilla and my dad to accomplish a greater purpose in me.

Not only did I get a new mom, but I also gained new aunts, uncles and grandparents. We were a culturally blended family being that my new family was of Puerto Rican and Irish descent. For some looking in, all they would probably see was a white lady raising a black child. Our family is much more than that. Race has never been an issue and we don't believe in "step." We believe that once you are in, you are in, and whatever family you come with becomes equivalent to a blood relative.

My new mom had four siblings so I gained two aunts and two uncles. Her younger sister was seven years older than me and her younger brother was five years older. Not only were her younger siblings my aunt and uncle but they also took on the role of godparents. I loved them dearly because to me an aunt and uncle represent second parents. Their instincts should be to love you as your parents love you and their concern should be for your best interest. The role of a "godparent" should be exactly what the word specifies, parents being led by God. Unfortunately, not every uncle or aunt sees themselves as second parents, and in today's society, a godparent has become a glorified title with no true commitment. I am not saying that they were bad godparents or even bad at being an aunt or uncle. They were more like older siblings and I loved them very much, just as they loved me.

When I first moved in with my parents we lived on Magnolia Street in a six-flat apartment building on the first floor. My aunt lived across the hall. Both of my parents worked and I was way too young to stay at home alone. My aunt had introduced my mom to her friend Sue and Ms. Sue became my babysitter for the summer.

Ms. Sue was a sassy white lady in her mid-thirties who was married to or just living with a Spanish man. She had blond straight hair and she smoked a lot. She lived a couple of blocks from us so it was very convenient for me to be there. I didn't mind going to Ms. Sue's house because she was a lot of fun. I seemed to have been the only one that Ms. Sue would babysit because I never really saw any other children at her house until that one day when a little white boy was there. I had never seen him before. He was about my age, maybe a year older. He had dirty blond hair and was on the thin side. He was a rowdy little boy with a little bit of a foul mouth. We had played the majority of the morning and Ms. Sue told us that we had to take a nap. Ms. Sue was in her room asleep and we were in the other room supposedly taking a nap but instead we were playing and jumping up and down on the bed. At one point we had just stopped jumping around and settled into lying down. All of sudden, the little boy rolled on top of me and started humping on me. I asked him what he was doing and he whispered in my ear, "I'm f---ing you". I didn't quite believe what he said so I asked him again and his reply was, "I'm f----ing you," as he continued to dry hump me. Once again I didn't know what to do or what to say. I just laid there. As I reminisce on that moment, I can only imagine the things that little boy was exposed to that caused him to perform such an act and then to verbalize it. I never saw that little boy again and I never told Ms. Sue or my mom what took place that day. I buried it.

I only spent the summer at Ms. Sue's house and in the fall my parents enrolled me in Our Lady of Mount Carmel Catholic School to attend third and fourth grade. Needless to say my transition from a predominately black public school to a multiracial Catholic school was a big adjustment. I was still dealing with anger, insecurity and abandonment, which manifested greatly in my behavior. I had never attended a school or associated with children of this caliber before. I was ghetto and they were not, so I had a very hard time adapting. I was not used to this type of structure so I did what I did best and acted out. I was not very well liked by the students and the teachers did not know what to do with me. This fact was expressed by my exhausted third grade teacher when my mom had her first parent teacher conference. That conference was the most embarrassing moment of her life. My mother left that conference wanting to crawl into a hole and retreat. When I came home that afternoon I received a whipping like I'd never received before. That was the last time we had that conversation.

Ultimately I began to adjust and make friends. I was still quite rambunctious but I had calmed down quite a bit from when I first arrived at Our Lady of Mount Carmel. In the end, I graduated the eighth grade from that school. It was the best school that I had ever attended, and I was fortunate enough to have met some of the most extraordinary friends of all backgrounds and cultures at a very young age. Some of my fondest school memories were at Mt. Carmel.

The summer before I was to attend the fifth grade we moved to 4413 N. Malden and this is where I spent my late childhood and teenage years. We moved into a three-bedroom apartment in a six flat building. As you walked in you were facing my parent's bedroom and to the left of their room was the living room that had an attached sunroom. My brother's bedroom was to the immediate right as you entered the front door and my bedroom was down the hall on the right. The apartment had a separate dining room, a large kitchen and one bathroom.

This apartment was the place where I experienced the joys and pains of my late childhood and teenage years. This particular dwelling was the heart of life for our family. Our greatest memories as well as some of our deepest woes occurred at this place of residence. Our home was the place where families gathered together for Christmas, birthdays and barbeques. This was the place where parties were held and life was lived. If you were to ask any member of my family, they would all agree that 4413 N. Malden was the best place that our family ever lived. But not only was this the place where there was much joy and pain and everyday living, this was also the place where those planted seeds from early on in my childhood were not only nurtured but this is where they blossomed. Many known and unknown things happened at 4413 N. Malden. Many secrets were birthed there.

CHAPTER 3

The Trespass

I have always loved my uncle. There was never a time, as a young girl, that I did not love him or want to be around him. My uncle was five years older than I so our age difference made it easy for me to look at him as a brother more so than an uncle.

I met him one time before my parents were married. They had picked me up from Geraldine's house one Easter Sunday and he was in the car waiting. He had to have been at least ten years old at the time. He was heavy in weight and looked like the typical white boy with glasses. When I got in the car, I really didn't pay much attention to him. I was too busy crying about leaving my mother and mad that my stuffed Easter bunny had fallen into the mud and was ruined as I was getting into the car. I can only imagine what his thoughts were about the crying child sitting next to him. I actually did not have a lot of contact with him after that initial meeting until my father and Cyrilla were married and I came to live with them. After that, I would see him when we would visit my grandmother's house or he would come to our apartment.

My uncle was the typical teenager. He listened to a lot of heavy metal music such as Kiss, Metallica and rock groups of that sort, and he loved horror movies. I remember going to the movies with him to see "Beyond the Door." This movie was about a pregnant woman possessed by the devil. He found it fascinating and it scared me terribly. The only thing I can remember from that horrid movie was a young lady getting slashed repeatedly and blood gushing everywhere. I don't know what made him think that this movie was appropriate for a child of my age. Knowing what I know now, a lot of spiritual doors were opened to his soul through the music he enjoyed and the movies that he watched.

When my family moved to 4413 N. Malden, I had completed the fourth grade and was entering into the fifth. A lot of changes were taking place that year for me. I was leaving my current Catholic grammar school to attend another public school. That alone was a lot to take in. I was ten years old and was also experiencing significant physical changes taking place in my body. I was beginning to develop into a preteen. My breasts were developing and my hips were taking form as well as my behind. I was starting to look a lot older physically than I actually was. I did not take great notice of this change until one night when someone else did.

The events that led up to that first illegal touch will always be imprinted on my mind. My uncle was staying at the house for a couple of days. He was around 16 years old at the time and I can imagine his hormones accompanied with the spirit of lust were the deciding factor of the occurrences that took place that evening. I don't know if he ever had sex with anyone before, but I guess he thought that I would be a good candidate to experiment with.

He was in the living room sitting in the big brown leather chair that was situated on the wall closest to the entrance of the living room. The television was in the corner to the left of the chair and if you were sitting in the chair you would have to turn your body to look at it. It was dark and the only light was the one coming from the television. I can't recall how many times I sat on my uncle's lap, if I ever sat on his lap at all; but as I walked into the living room and looked around searching for a suitable seat, I found myself nonchalantly maneuvering myself so that I was resting comfortably on his left thigh with my back against his chest. While sitting there I had no fear or apprehension because he had never given me a reason to feel those things.

We were sitting there watching television and as we sat I felt his right hand slightly brush my right breast. This touch was subtle and appeared to be nonthreatening. He did not attempt to move his hand under my shirt but continued to caress my right breast through my clothing. This type of interaction had never taken place between us before so I did not know how to process what was going on. No one had ever taken the time to teach me about physical boundaries and what was considered to be a "good" touch or a "bad" touch so my instincts did not tell me to jump up and run to the back where my parents were. After all, he was my uncle and why would he hurt me or do anything to me that was wrong, so I just sat there as he continued to fondle me. As I sat there, time stood still and all I could do was stare at the television.

It felt weird while I was sitting on his lap with his hand touching and squeezing my right breast, as I stared dumbfounded at the television, for what appeared to be a lifetime. There were no words exchanged during the incident nor was there anything said after. As I got up from his lap, I don't believe we made any eye contact. My uncle did not come out and say it but the communication that was taking place was screaming, "Hush, don't tell our secret." As I walked to my bedroom, I did not know that the unspoken agreement between my uncle and I would be the beginning of more hidden secrets.

I woke up the next morning not quite knowing how to feel about what took place the night before. However, I was a little apprehensive about being around my uncle. He had spent the night and was in the living room on the floor asleep, or so I thought. My parents had already left for work so we were alone in the house.

That day I had worn a pair of jeans with my favorite blue two-toned, short sleeved sweater with a dark blue owl on it. I remember this outfit so well because it is what I was wearing when my uncle's subtleness evolved into sheer boldness. Maybe it was because I did not say anything or react the night before that made him think he had the right to pursue his 10-year-old niece as means of sexual gratification. Maybe my silence gave him the impression that it was permissible for him to do what he did. It very well could have been that he had pondered on his actions all night and lust had captivated him and convinced him to see me, his niece, not as the child that I was, but as an object of his lust. Nor did he see himself as an uncle who was supposed to protect. Whatever the reason may have been, what he did next was the beginning of a trespass that no child should ever suffer.

I was getting ready to leave to go to school that morning and my uncle called me into the living room. He must have been thinking about what he was going to do all night because he seemed to have awakened from his sleep just to catch me before I walked out the door. My parents had already left out for work so it just left him and me in the house.

As I walked into the living room, he grabbed me and laid me down on my back in front of the fireplace. As I was lying there he lifted up my shirt and the part of my bra that covered my right breast, placed his mouth on my breast and began to suck on it. As he did that, he fondled the left. As he placed his mouth on my breast my mind went to another place. I was in the midst of what was going on physically but I was trying to escape mentally. Again, just as the night before, I did not yell or protest but I felt that this was not supposed to be taking place. When he let me up, once again there was an unspoken agreement that stated the incident that had just taken place was not to be repeated to anyone. Afterwards, I gathered myself and left for school.

That day in school it was as if I was floating in a dream. I sat in my seat and literally covered myself by placing my left arm clear across my chest and securing my left hand safely under my right armpit to ensure that nothing would penetrate. I sat in that protective stance throughout the day staring into space. I was physically in the classroom but my mind was on what took place on that living room floor just a few hours ago. Not only was the scene playing over and over in my mind, I could still feel the wetness of his mouth on me.

As I was walking home, I knew that my uncle would be there waiting, sitting in that big brown leather chair. Somehow I knew that this was the beginning of something that I did not know how to stop. Why didn't I cry out or protest? How was I supposed to feel about what had taken place? Why did he do this to me? There were all these big questions bombarding the mind of a ten-year-old child, questions that I could not begin to answer. I felt dirty and unclean. I walked home slowly as I could, trying to avoid the inevitable. When I got home, he was waiting in that big brown leather chair. He had that look in his eye as he beckoned me to come and sit on his lap.

That big brown leather chair was the root and the birthplace of all evil deeds. That chair was the place where the unspeakable occurred between an uncle and his niece. These illegal acts were performed between a teenage boy and a very young girl. It was the place where a predator committed a crime against his victim.

Those two incidents marked the place where boundaries had been crossed and the death of an uncle and niece relationship took place. The events that occurred in that twelve-hour time frame forever altered my life. I really don't think that he ever knew how much his actions affected me mentally, emotionally, and physically. I believe that he was so empowered by his own lust and sexual desires that all reasoning had gone and he turned his niece into some sort of a sex toy. At least that's how I was beginning to feel.

With each episode I began to associate myself with the cheap women that I saw on the pornographic movies that we had viewed from time to time. Often I would sneak and watch the pornographic movies and further invite that lustful spirit in. That perverse spirit was making its way deeper into my soul through the things that I watched and the illegal soul tie that was forming between my uncle and me.

It seemed that every opportunity my uncle had he found a way to fondle me or to put his hands down my pants. His advances graduated as time progressed and he began to do things to me that would resemble acts from the pornographic movies we watched. Lasciviousness and lust ruled and I was the object of that vile affection.

My goal is not to relive every illicit act that was done to me, for there were many, but to give an idea of how the enemy will use those closest to you to take you out. The enemy's agenda was to cause fragmentation to my soul early on in my life so that I would be a dysfunctional adult. He used my uncle, who was dealing with a lot of soul perverseness himself, as a conduit to carry out his plans.

The molestation went on for many years. I can say that every act from fondling, caressing, probing my vagina with his fingers, and oral sex to watching him masturbate as he touched me was the full extent of this trespass. Fortunately, there was never a time when intercourse took place.

The more he did it, the more he wanted to do it. The more he did it, the more I felt cheapened but I would bury and ignore that feeling. I never understood why I never protested. Why was this acceptable behavior for me? There were times when I objected but the objection was more that of a girlfriend not wanting to be bothered by a boyfriend rather than a child wanting to be free of her sexually abusive uncle. What was in me that was becoming adjusted and even conforming to this type of attention and what was in me that was beginning to want this attention? What was causing my body to respond to a touch that should have been repulsive to me?

I had become used to this type of activity every time my uncle was around. There was never a time that we were in each other's presence that he did not find a way to touch me. My family would be in the dining room playing cards and he would be in the living room sitting in that big brown chair with me on his lap; his hand up my blouse and his other hand between my legs. If we heard someone coming down the hall, he would immediately shove me off his lap. I often wondered if anyone had any idea of what was taking place. How could this be happening right in front of them and no one have a clue?

I remember one time while sitting on his lap, as he was touching me, I asked him, "Is this a sin?" and without hesitation he said, "Yes it is." His response did not stir a sense of awareness to what was taking place to propel him to stop nor did it initiate any sign of regret. He just continued to fondle me as if the question had not been asked.

I sit today and think about that response and the lack of reaction to the response on his part, I know now that I had a conversation with the devil.

CHAPTER 4

An Illegal Relationship
(From Molestation to Incest)

Webster defines molestation as to make indecent sexual advances to, to assault sexually. When someone thinks of a sexual assault, one may immediately think of a violent attack of rape. Attack is defined as to set upon in a forceful, violent, hostile or aggressive way. In my case, the assault of molestation was not violent nor could it be considered physically hostile. It was a subtle invasion that began with one touch.

This assault did not happen on a deserted dark street or in the back of an alley from an unknown aggressor who instilled terror. Instead, this assault was much worse. This offense came with a smile and at the hand of someone who was trusted, loved, and who held the role of protector. It was not threatening nor did the attack leave me physically battered or scarred. This attack was much worse because it was an emotional assassination. What this intrusion did was awaken and nurture the sexual seed of corruption that was implemented earlier on in childhood. With each encounter, that seed grew roots that went deeper into my mind and emotions which ultimately affected my will. I had a twisted perception of my relationship with my uncle that caused me to feed into the terrible lie that what was transpiring between us was "okay." And as wretched as it was, I began to accept it as normal and with acceptance came a level of participation and consent.

The physical intimacy happened so many times that it became the norm, if you can understand that. It was what we did when we were together. Every incident turned into something sexual. A simple game of monopoly resulted in some physical interaction. Even the times that I would ask him for something simple and innocent, it had to result in a sexual favor. The times that I did not comply, he acted like a mad boyfriend and would not speak to me and literally ignored me. This is how we interacted and this was our relationship.

A prime example of accepting this behavior as the "norm" is clearly illustrated in the movie "Precious." Precious had been molested and raped by her father since she was a small child. She never had a boyfriend and her sexual experiences were only with her father. She had conceived two children by him. One day, while sitting in class, after finding out she had tested positive for HIV, the reality of her situation and her brokenness came crashing down as she uttered, "My father promised that he was going to marry me but all I got was raped, beaten, and sick." Even though she knew that he was her father and on some level it had to be "not right," it became the norm for her to the point that she had anticipated marriage. Her sexual relationship with her father was the only relationship she had with him, so that was all she knew. He was not the man who took on the role of protector, but rather he embraced the role of predator.

The interaction that my uncle and I had with one another resembled that of a couple instead of family members. What this had become was an immoral bond birthed from corruption and lust. An uncle became a boyfriend and a niece became a girlfriend. One touch evolved into a relationship that was illegal, perverse, and depraved.

Molestation is a vile crime against a child. This crime leaves a child in an emotional state that will forever impact his or her life. But what happens when the sin of molestation graduates into the consenting sin of incest? When those lines begin to blur, at some point the victim becomes a participating victim. I know some may not agree with this statement so please let me explain. A participating victim is one who willing participates in a situation that continually victimizes them. It is no longer a predator taking complete advantage of his prey, but his prey has accepted, on some level, come into agreement with the actions of the trespass. I say this because at a certain age one can distinguish between what is right and what is wrong and becomes accountable for their actions. As a child, one is incapable of defending themselves and is easily intimidated as well as manipulated into complying. In my case, as I got older – going into my teenage years, there should have been something in me to say that this is not right and it must stop.

I can't recall exactly when I crossed the line and went from victim to a participating victim. I do know that this transformation did not take long for me to come into agreement with this sexual sin. At the time, I did not look at it as sin because I didn't really know what sin was. I knew that what we were doing was something that was not to be announced up on the rooftop, but I had no spiritual concept of what sin really was. I did not have a relationship with Christ and neither did my parents so it was very easy for that spirit of perversion to invade our home and comfortably rest. Although I did not know about the act of incest being a sin, for the most part I did not know what incest was, but deep down inside, I knew that it was not right.

Because we had indulged in these incestuous acts for quite some time, I became very accustomed to it and sad to say, began to physically enjoy it. It is amazing what our physical man, our flesh, will enjoy that our spirit and soul will loath. I was going through puberty at the time and my body was awakened to a lot of physical changes and desires. The touching and caressing caused an amount of stimulation that was pleasing. That, coupled with my spirit being polluted with pornography, a spiritual door had been opened to lust. Not only was it physically gratifying but also on some level it was becoming emotionally gratifying.

It became emotionally gratifying to me because I secretly enjoyed the attention that I was receiving. I was not the prettiest girl growing up and to be dark skinned in my day was hard. Most boys my age liked the slim shaped girls with the caramel colored skin and the long straight hair. Girls like me, dark skinned with an overdeveloped body, did not have much of a chance. That was reinforced by the many guys that I liked who always fell for my friends. The fear of not being liked enforced that feeling of rejection, which was an open spiritual door that the enemy used against me to aid in my compliance. My uncle provided the attention that I was craving and because we were so close in age, it was like having a boyfriend.

This incestuous relationship went on for five years. I was ten years old, in the fifth grade, when the first incident took place, and I was about fifteen when it came to an end. During that time I was exposed to pornography, taught how to masturbate and climax, and how to use sex when dealing with men. My uncle taught me well. Although intercourse never took place between us, he suggested it one time by telling me he had a condom in his wallet. Even with all that was going on, I knew that would be crossing a very sick line and there would be no way I could explain if I became pregnant. After all, I was at an age where I was not yet permitted to have a boyfriend.

In the years that my uncle and I had this affair, like any other girlfriend, I came and went. There was one time when I was introduced to one of his girlfriends. I can't recall her name but I do remember that she was a victim of a sexual assault in her life. I found it quite odd that he introduced me to her and told me about her abuse, when in fact, he was an abuser himself. There was even a time that he wanted to date one of my girlfriends and asked me if I was interested in his friend. In the end, we would always resume our relationship and he would come to me for "comfort."

This "comfort" happened once when he and a girlfriend had broken up and he came over to our house to spend the night. His approach to me was one who had been wounded, heartbroken and just needed someone to care. There I was, again, lying on the floor with his hand up my shirt and his hand down my pants. At one point the touching evolved into grinding. He was rubbing himself against me and penetration almost occurred. After that incident, for a few days I was in a panic because my mind kept telling me that I was pregnant. Although I was not ignorant as to how babies were made, in my mind, the near penetration was a form of intercourse and the fear of it all weighed heavily on me. After all, the explanation of how I got pregnant and especially with whom, would have been a devastating ordeal. I never brought my scare to his attention because I knew he would think that I was stupid and probably blow it off.

What I found most interesting about my uncle is how he would take on the role of a "concerned" uncle and inquire if I had these type of relationship with anyone else. My response was always no, because I wasn't allowed to have a boyfriend or even date. Funny how an uncle's role is to protect, but he was protective in the wrong type of way. He wasn't being protective because he was looking out for my best interest and didn't want me to be taken advantage of. That concerned had died when he crossed the line with that first touch. His main concern was that he wanted to ensure he was the only one who had those privileges. It was a concern born out of selfish intentions and self-seeking motives.

For anyone looking in, no one would look at us and think that we had anything other than a "normal" uncle and niece relationship. Our secret was very well hidden. We had become very good actors and simulated a normal relationship that a niece and an uncle would have and no one was the wiser. I got so accustomed to masking and hiding that I began to lose myself in the charade. I did not understand what I was doing or why I was doing it. There were times that I wanted it to stop but I did not know how to make it stop. I went on with everyday life year after year as if nothing was happening, or so I thought. Little did I know that spiritually I was being setup to become an emotionally dysfunctional adult. I was locked into a relationship that was causing me nothing but shame and emotional distress. I did not know how distressed I was because I refused to acknowledge the inner cry inside of me. Instead, I laid that cry in a coffin to rest and buried it in the deepest part of my soul.

The connection I had with my uncle was the biggest injustice I had experienced up to that point in my life and it was the biggest lie I had ever told to myself. This relationship was designed to birth a perverted covenant and an ungodly soul tie that would keep me emotionally attached to him long after it had ended.

CHAPTER 5

The Relentless Soul Tie

The other night I was sitting in my living room watching television. As I went through the menu I saw that the movie, "Flowers in the Attic" and soon after "Petals in the Wind" would be coming on. These two movies were birthed from a book by V.C. Andrews. I read those books as a teenager and I was interested to see if the television version would do justice to the story line.

The movie was about a young woman named Corrine Dahl and her four children. Corrine had lost her husband and was forced to gather her four children Christopher, Cathy, Cory and Carrie and go back to live with her parents at Foxworth Hall. Corrine's parents disowned her because she had fallen in love with and married her father's younger half-brother, Christopher Dahl. Both parents stood very firm that their incestuous relationship was unclean and unholy, so Corrine and her half uncle, Christopher, ran away, married and built a life together for sixteen years. With the sudden unexpected death of her husband due to a car accident, Corrine had no choice but to go home to try to win back her father's affections and be placed back into his will to gain the family fortune. In order to achieve this, she had to keep her children that were born from her unholy union with her uncle, a secret from her father.

Corrine and her mother devised a plan to lock her children in the attic just long enough to win back her dying father's love. What was supposed to have been a couple of weeks of hiding turned into two years that these children were locked in the attic and in those two years a lot transpired.

There is nothing like the love between a brother and sister, especially when they are there to help each other get through traumatic times. The bond that is formed is unbreakable. Christopher, the oldest son, and Cathy, the second oldest, grew very close during their time of captivity. They went from being a brother and sister to becoming a father and mother to the younger twins Cory and Carrie, but their relationship went far beyond that. They had been locked in an attic for two years and during that time they became very conscious of the physical changes in their bodies and began to take notice of each other. Both were becoming very aware of their sexuality. Because of the circumstances that they had been placed in, they turned to each other when their curiosity and desire had overtaken them. Although they knew it was wrong, they experienced their first sexual experience with one another.

"Flowers in the Attic" ends with Christopher, Cathy and Carrie (Cory dies) escaping from the attic. The story picks up in "Petals in the Wind" and places you in their lives 15 years after their escape from the horrors of the attic. Even though Christopher and

Cathy try to move on from the incestuous relationship that took place fifteen years prior, their attempts are futile and they find themselves still very much drawn to each other in a way that no sister and brother should be. Both go on to pursue their careers, Christopher as a doctor and Cathy as a professional ballet dancer, but find it difficult to be without one another. Christopher finds it extremely difficult to see Cathy any other way than as a lover and even though Cathy had married (her husband dies in a car accident) and had children, her attraction to her brother was greater than her. People that were around them could detect their unique closeness and their need one for the other. No matter how hard they tried or how much they knew it was wrong, they were drawn to each other. At one point in the story, Christopher gets engaged in an attempt to move on but in the end, when his fiancé caught him kissing Cathy, he knew that his heart forever belonged to his sister. In the end, Christopher and Cathy, (Carrie commits suicide) move to another state where no one knows their true identities, and they marry and have children. The very same thing that their parents did, they also did. The very tie, although wrong, that held their parents together, held them together. It was a replication of a sinful cycle.

"Flowers in the Attic" and "Petals in the Wind" depict dreadful accounts of physical and emotional abuse, psychological torment, and ungodly soul ties conceived through incest. In the beginning, Christopher and Cathy shared the pure bond that a typical brother and sister would normally share. The bond that knitted them together as siblings was corrupted through their incestuous relationship which birth an ungodly soul tie or bond.   The soul tie they shared was the kind meant only for a husband and wife. In the end, their connection was so strong that it prevented them from having a life with anyone else outside of each other.   And although they knew intellectually it was wrong, their emotions were so twisted and entwined with each other that they viewed their wrong as right and married and raised children together, hence keeping the spiritual door open for the spirit of perversion to go from generation to generation as seen in the sequels "Seeds of Yesterday" and "If there be Thorns."

A soul tie is a very powerful connection. It develops when two souls are knitted (interwoven) together connecting them spiritually and them becoming one flesh. Soul ties are formed through godly and ungodly sexual relations, vows, commitments, and agreements. Sexual relations are the most common practice where soul ties develop. Let's take a look at the difference between godly and ungodly unions.

Godly Sexual Relations:

A godly sexual soul tie is formed between a man and a woman in marriage; Ephesians 5:31, *"For this cause shall a man leave his father and mother, and shall be joined unto his wife, and they two shall be one flesh" (KJV).* This bond, which is intended by God, is unbreakable by man and will draw the husband and wife closer together which will result in a stronger union. Because marriage is the order that God intended for man and woman to co-habitat together, when we follow that order, blessings will flow from God to us. Any sexual relations outside of marriage is defiled in the eyes of God, Hebrews 13:4, *"Let marriage be held in honor by all, and the bed undefiled: but fornicators and adulterers God will judge (KJV).* God gave us the gift of sex. It is the natural affection between a husband and wife. It draws them close and cultivates intimacy.

Ungodly Sexual Relations:

Ungodly soul ties, such as that shared between people indulging in sex outside of marriage in the form of fornication, adultery, incest, rape, or molestation, places the soul in slavery; I Corinthians 6:16, *"What? Know ye not that he which is joined to a harlot is one body? For "Two, saith he, shall be one flesh (KJV)".*

An ungodly soul tie is very destructive and causes fragmentation and hardship to the soul. This type of soul tie is very influential and has a tenacious grip on the emotions. It keeps the soul in captivity to the other person. You see this type of hold when an abused wife keeps going back to an abusive husband. This bond is so strong that murders, called crimes of passion, have been committed. An ungodly soul tie will cause a husband or wife to leave the security and covenant of their marriage to pursue the uncertain and indulge in the forbidden fruit of adultery.

When we engage in sexual relations outside of the order of God's plan, not only are we spiritually connecting to the person that we are engaging sexually with, but we also become spiritually connected with those whom our partner has previously engaged in sexual activity with. So, we are not only sleeping with them, but we are sleeping with and becoming one with everyone that they have slept with.

Engaging in sex is just not a physical act. Sex penetrates the emotions and ignite our feelings. Once our feelings are ignited, if not careful, they can lead us to think and react in an unhealthy and irrational way. Ungodly sexual relations are very dangerous because when two souls that are tied together separate, the souls are torn causing devastation. Resentment, bitterness, and hurt are often the result of that tearing. The soul becomes severely damaged when the process is repeated such as chasing one relationship after another. Literally, fragments of the soul (our mind and emotions) are scattered and pieces are attached to many people. It takes the work of Holy Spirit to sever and to release us from the bondage of ungodly soul ties.

Abuse in any form is a weapon that Satan uses to destroy people mentally, physically, and emotionally. Sexual abuse is the most destructive because it enslaves the soul, twists and damages the emotions, bombards the mind with lies, and causes one to feel unloved, self-hate, shame, guilt, and condemnation. The soul ties born from such abuse keeps the abused attached to the abuser like an umbilical cord keeps a baby joined to its mother. While in the womb, the umbilical cord is necessary in order for the baby to live. In order for the baby to survive outside of the womb of the mother, that cord must be severed. The same is true of spiritual soul ties. While in the relationship (the womb), the soul feeds off the activity of that relationship. Once one is delivered out of the relationship, in order for one to be free from the emotional attachment of the one they have indulged in illegal sexual relations with, the spiritual cord must be cut.

The relationship that my uncle and I shared went on from the time I was in fifth grade until I was a freshman in high school. At the age of sixteen I was permitted to have a boyfriend and my uncle was most likely dating as well. The encounters that we shared began to dwindle and became less frequent. It seems that as we got older, there was less time that we spent together. The times in which we were together we were surrounded by family and it seemed that there was no "alone" time. However, the times that we were alone, nothing would transpire between us. I did not know how to take this change in activity because it was all that I knew. Is was as if a boyfriend was losing interest and I did not know what to do to keep his attention. I found myself pursuing him because there was an unexplainable pull to him and a desire for him.

What I was feeling, the yearning and that pull to him, although perverted, was that ungodly soul tie, the spiritual umbilical cord. It was the knitting together of our souls that had developed through the molestation and the incest. This soul tie kept me emotionally and physically attached to him. The desire for him was so strong that from time to time I would find myself masturbating and calling out his name as I reached a climax. The grip of perversion was so strong and the soul tie was so deep that my mind and emotions perceived him as my lover.

Our relationship was in a transitional stage and it became very apparent that things were changing. That change became evident when my uncle was at our house for a weekend. I was lying on the couch in the living room watching television as he sat in that big brown leather chair reading the newspaper. Whenever he sat in that chair I knew that it would not be long before he would call me over to come sit on his lap. That is how everything would always start. He would sit in the brown chair, call my name and beckon to me, but something was different this day. I was watching television and I found myself looking back at him as if to say "when are you going to call me?" We had been in the room alone for quite some time and there were no advances made. I was laying there waiting for him to call my name and when my name was not called I felt a deep sense of rejection. I should have been relieved that he ignored me, but that was not the case. I felt like a jilted girlfriend who had given away her most prized possession and then got tossed aside. I had no idea why I felt that way; after all, I should have been thankful that he didn't take this opportunity to touch me, but that wasn't the situation at all. I wanted him to beckon me to sit on his lap. For some odd reason that was the only connection that I had with him and it was a connection, strangely enough, I did not want to be broken.

Because of the ungodly sexual relationship that my uncle and I shared, our souls had become so connected that the sudden breaking of that bond caused emotional damage. Feelings of rejection and abandonment was once again awakened in me. Although intercourse did not occur, our bond had been formed through kissing, oral sex, and fondling, which often resulted in sexual climax. We were connected in a way that was described by Paul in I Corinthians 6:16. That connection left me wounded and alone to bear the aftermath of the trespass, but not only that, that connection had opened many demonic spiritual doors and gave the enemy legal access to my life.

CHAPTER 6

Spiritual Doors

Win Worley, a dedicated evangelist and a powerful deliverer, speaks profoundly about how the enemy will disrupt a child's life through the spirit of Arrested Development. Arrested Development is a strongman that gains legal access in a child's life through trauma. This ruling spirit and the strong-holds (spirits that are linked to the ruling spirit) that accompany this spirit are assigned to disrupt the mental and emotional maturing of a person. This spirit is most effective in children if access is gained before the age of nine.

In his teaching, "Arrested Development," Win reveals how the enemy's agenda is to arrest (stop progress of), the development (the process of growing) of our mind, will, and emotions so our thought process will remain in child-like state. This arresting causes us to deal with situations and circumstances as an adult with a childlike mindset. It also confuses the child's mind when it comes to their sexuality and may cause a young girl to take on mannish behavior while a boy may exhibit feminine behavior, leaving the spiritual door open to embrace homosexuality and lesbianism. Arrested Development is designed to manipulate and distort the mind. The events that pave the way for the arrested development spirits to enter in are severe trauma, abuse, incest, molestation, loneliness, fear, severe rejection, abandonment rebellion, and lack of discipline.

My soul was opened to the spirit of Arrested Development because of the emotional and sexual trauma that I was exposed to as a child. The circumstances surrounding the broken relationship with my mother, Geraldine, and the things that I witnessed her do and ultimately the molestation that took place all played major roles in ushering in that spirit.

Our soul consists of our mind, our will, and our emotions. Satan's agenda is to cause fragmentation and brokenness to these areas. He uses spiritual doors, which are entrances to gain admittance to us. If he is successful in inflicting wounds to any part of our soul, he gains influence over our lives and causes us to live a life of poor and unhealthy behavior.

There are many ways that spiritual doors can be opened. Our eyes (what we see), our ears (what we hear), and our mouth (what we speak) are gates that are used for access. You have heard the expression, "the eyes are the windows to the soul"; that statement rings true. What we look at feeds our soul and spirit. If we are constantly using our eye gate to view pornography, we are opening a spiritual door and inviting the spirit of lust and perversion to come in. If one is exposed to wrong behavior, such as a child witnessing a father beat their mother, that action is imprinted on the mind of the child. If it is a son witnessing the abuse, he may become an abuser. If a girl is constantly witnessing her mother being abused, she may accept that same behavior as an adult.

As a child, I saw my mother, Geraldine, endure abuse at the hand of her boyfriend. That image was embedded in my thoughts and caused me to unconsciously form an opinion about what relationships were like. Although I never endured physical abuse from a companion, I allowed a certain amount of emotional and verbal abuse to take place.

It is the same with our ear gates. What we listen to affects us as well. For instance, listening to music or viewing movies that have a lot of profanity opens the door to the spirit of profanity to rest in us. If not careful, we will find ourselves using profanity as well. The enemy also uses our ear gates to plant negative seeds about who we are. When we constantly hear negative things about ourselves we begin to accept and embody that negative character. We unconsciously come into agreement with what has been spoken to us and over us and begin to operate in it. For example, if a child continues to hear how bad he/she is and that he/she will never amount to anything, those words that he/she hears will begin to take root in his/her mind and emotions and his or her actions will demonstrate what the mind and emotions have taken in. What we are consistently exposed to has a way of manifesting in us.

Our mouth is a gate that the enemy likes to dominate. The Bible tells us in James 3:8 *"But the tongue can no man tame; it is an unruly evil, full of deadly poison" (KJV).* Words have power and what we speak has a negative or positive impact on us.

Genesis 1 is a rich illustration of the power of words when God spoke everything but man into existence. Proverbs 18:21, tells us *"Death and life are In the power of the tongue and those who love it will eat its fruit" (KJV)*. Our world is formed with the words that we speak. When we speak negativity we are releasing those words to take root in our lives and eventually we come into agreement, through our actions, with the words that we've spoken. If we are constantly speaking defeat, poverty, and lack, then we will live a life of defeat, poverty, and lack.

Satan uses our eye, ear, and mouth gates to open up spiritual doors because they provide direct access to the soul. Remember, his plan is to shatter the mind and emotions which will greatly influence our behavior.

The mind is the main area where Satan attacks. The mind is a battlefield and there is a constant war raging for the well-being and peace of it. Proverbs 4:23 admonishes us to *"Keep thy heart with all diligence; for out of it flows the issues of life" (KJV)*. The Hebrew word for heart is *leb* (Strong's 3820) and is defined as the seat of thought, mind and understanding. Our mind is a prime target for Satan because our mind (heart) is the seat of our intellect, emotions, will and moral consciousness. We form our thoughts and attitudes about people, situations, circumstances, and ourselves in our mind; and if negatively influenced, our perception can deviate from that of the norm.

Satan tenaciously seeks to place strongholds (an area where an enemy dominates) in our mind and any area where there is a stronghold, the enemy controls. When Satan gains control over our thoughts, he is able to rule our attitude. He convinces us of a lie about ourselves, which causes us to live the opposite of what God has designed for us. He is the father of lies and his lies rob us of the truth of who God says we are and the promises that he has for us. His agenda is to strip us of our true identity, our true self, which originates from God.

For those of us who have been abused, these lies cause us to develop a bad attitude about any and all things that pertain to us. This attitude will often make us feel worthless and insecure and these characteristics will manifest in our everyday life. His desire is to keep us mentally bound by and connected to the hurt and the shame of the abuse. He deceives us by convincing us that we are everything that the abuse stood for, thus keeping us in a victim mindset.

That is what I was. I was a victim of my circumstances. I was suffering the consequences from someone else's actions. My mind was disrupted at an early age and I began to form an opinion about myself that was not who God really intended me to be. The enemy had stolen my God-given identity and replaced it with a false identity of worthlessness and I willingly embraced that lie.

Emotions are also a prime target for the enemy. Our feelings, if not harnessed, can control us. When our emotions have been wounded we have the tendency to become emotional thinkers and reactors. This is what the enemy wants because in our emotional state he can control us like a puppet on a string.

The emotional trauma from the estranged relationship that I had with my mother, Geraldine, was an open gateway for rejection, insecurity, abandonment, and a feeling of worthlessness that took a hold of me. The parent is the first teacher of the child and what that parent imparts is what that child embraces. I embraced a tainted love from a mother who did not understand that her actions were molding my perception of life. She left me and that's all that I knew. I knew nothing of the reasons why we were no longer together, all I knew was that I had a mother and she was taken away from me. I had a love that should have been unconditional but I was not her choice; she yielded to the spirit that had her captured. She was in bondage and bondage is what she passed down.

Not only did I lose a mother but I also lost a sister that was so very dear to me. The separation from the two most important people in my young life caused a brokenness and a certain type of emotional death. Because of the rejection and the abandonment, my emotions were so twisted that I welcomed all that insecurity, low self-esteem, and feelings of insignificance had to offer me. I made a covenant (agreement) with these negative emotions and held them close to me. I walked hand-in-hand with these emotions daily and allowed them to dictate who I was in life.

The spiritual door to sexual perversion was opened before the actual trespass of molestation took place. This door was opened when I was living with my grandmother and I had a dream-type vision of a man and a woman having sex on the coffee table. As he penetrated her, I physically felt the penetration. I was being spiritually raped. That experience set the stage for sexual corruption to manifest throughout my life.

I realize now that a sexual demon was assigned to me early on in life. This may be hard for some of you to fully understand but it is imperative that we realize we are spiritual as well as natural beings and that we are engaged in a spiritual war from the time that we are born into this world until the time that we leave this world. Satan's aim is to cripple us emotionally so that we can be flawed throughout our life. His agenda is for our lives to produce the strange fruit of sin instead of the sweet aroma of righteousness.

There are many incidents that took place that set me up for destruction. In looking back into my childhood I can see where the enemy would want me to be ashamed and cause that "hush don't tell" spirit to overtake me. Now I know what God has done for me and this testimony is for me not to succumb to shame and defeat, but to help someone come out of the jail cell of condemnation and shame; to break the silence and expose the secrets that have been kept for generations and to issue a warning to the enemy that our bloodline and the generations to come will no longer be tainted by that foul spirit of perversion. It is time for us to rest in the sweet freedom that Jesus Christ has for us and to rebuke the lies that the enemy has kept us enslaved.

Webster defines the word "to pervert" as to cause to turn aside or away from what is good or true or morally right. One thing that perversion does is to convince you that what is wrong is right and what is right is wrong. It distorts the truth and the lie becomes a reality. It is only a lie and there is no truth to it but because you believe it, in your mind, it is your reality. When a spiritual door is opened to perversion, the mind and will seek those things that are immoral and unnatural.

One of the doors that the enemy opened up to me was that of lesbianism. This door was cracked during the time that I caught Geraldine in the bed with the man and the woman. This spiritual door was also opened with my childhood best friend. My best friend and I grew up together because my father and her father were good friends. I was always happy to go with my dad to their house because we would have so much fun. She was a rebel and we seemed to always get into mischief together.

I don't know when it first happened or how it came about or who approached whom but we started to engage in sexual acts together. We did not know anything about lesbianism or what it meant to be gay. It was not a confession that we knew to make and quite frankly that type of interaction was not as acceptable as it is today. We were at an age where we should not have known about sex at all but for some reason that curiosity was very heavy on the both of us. What we did know was that it was a means of experimenting and that the act, although we had an idea that it was wrong, felt physically good. Although naïve in our mind, there was a twisted perception of sexuality, the act in and of itself was a setup from the enemy for us to be spiritually arrested by that spirit of lesbianism so that we would embrace and take that twisted desire for the same sex into our adulthood sexuality. But by the grace of God, that spirit of lesbianism did not take root and manifest in our adulthood as the enemy had desired.

Because I had experienced these things at an age where emotional, mental, and physical development were taking place, Satan was setting me up to indulge in a life that was not ordained by God. He had placed those spiritual strongholds on me at a young age in order to accomplish that.

The sexual exploitation allowed me to become well acquainted with sin, condemnation, guilt, shame, and the feeling of uncleanliness to the point that I had labeled myself a worthless whore. These feelings became very real to me as I stood in the mirror, after an intimate moment with my boyfriend, and called myself a whore. As I looked in that mirror I saw every sexual act that I had indulged in willingly or not and I saw ugliness and self-hatred and I embraced it. As I stared at my reflection, I saw someone who was taken advantage of and then thrown away like a frayed doll. A shattered child was the reflection that glared back at me. A tattered little girl in need was buried deep inside me screaming to get out. As I stared back at this screaming child, this suffering child, my soul said, "hush, it will be alright, you are fine," and I donned my mask of self-deception.

CHAPTER 7

The Tattered Little Girl

As I stared in the mirror and looked at the girl staring back at me, I convinced her that she would be okay. Whatever okay looked like, I was determined to be. In essence, I was lying to myself. I was literally setting myself up to fall. The silencing of the hurting child caused me to suppress a lot of things. By my teenage years I was dealing with so many mixed emotions about myself and I was not equipped to handle any of them. I put up a front that all was well but deep down inside there was a struggle going on and I was losing the battle.

There had been so many times that I wanted to reveal to my mother what had gone on between my uncle and I but I did not have the heart to do so. I remember one evening my mother and I were in the kitchen and she was cleaning off the counter. I laid my head on her shoulder and began to silently weep. It was a muffled cry and she had no idea that I was crying. I thought that this would be the time that I could release what I had been holding but something held me back. I did not know how to tell her because I did not know how it would disrupt our family. That was the last thing I wanted to do was to cause any friction within the family. I knew that the news would break her heart and I knew that my father would have probably gone to jail for attempted murder. So I decided to forever keep it a secret by placing that injured little girl in a spiritual coffin, nailing it shut, and burying her hurt deep within my soul. In doing so, the anguish that I felt manifested itself in other ways.

At a very young age, my thought process had been arrested and my perception of myself, relationships, friendships, sex, and especially men was tainted. I did not know how to interact with men outside of a sexual manner. I did not know how to relate to a male in a platonic way. It was hard for me to distinguish between the two. The strongman of Arrested Development and all that accompanied it had become very comfortable within me. As a result, I suffered greatly with anger, insecurity, self-doubt, manipulation, control, rejection, people-pleasing, and sabotage. These spirits were the driving forces in my life and manifested in my actions.

Once I was allowed to date, I started to date Chris Barton. We met in downtown Chicago one Saturday afternoon. My girlfriends and I were on the bus and he and his friends were on the corner across the street. We happened to wave at each other and my friends and I decided to get off the bus and speak to them. That was the beginning of our relationship.

Chris really liked me and there wasn't anything that he wouldn't do for me. My parents also liked him so he was able to come around a lot. He was the first young man that I experienced sexual intercourse with. He was also the first young man that I told about what took place between my uncle and I. I told him because there would be times that we would be kissing and touching, the very thing that young teenagers in "love" do, and I would have flash backs about being with my uncle and abruptly stop. At that time, I had come to the full understanding that the relations I'd had with my uncle were very wrong and the consequences of those actions resulted in a deep-seated anger that I was beginning to feel towards him. Chris understood and was actually a great support. He had actually met my uncle and had liked him but from the moment that I revealed the secret of our relationship, Chris had lost any respect that he had for him and really had a hard time being in his presence without wanting to do physical harm to him.

Not only was Chris understanding about my sometimes abrupt reaction toward him but he was very supportive when I had gained the courage to call my uncle and ask him why he did what he did to me. Not really knowing what answer to expect from my uncle, the answer that I received was "It just happened and sorry." That was not the answer that I needed to hear. In fact, that answer left me stunned and screaming on the other end of the line, but no matter what my reaction was, all I heard was the cool nonchalant voice of my perpetrator on the other end. I later found out that he answered that way because his mother - my grandmother - was in the room and he really couldn't give an in-depth answer as to why he did what he did. Although his nonchalant answer was his attempt to hide the truth from my grandmother, I believe that on some level she knew or suspected because it would have been a situation that she would have been familiar with.

Chris was the type of boyfriend that we would consider as a "keeper," but I did not want to keep him. We dated for two years and in that time I expressed many character traits to him. On one hand I could be very loving and caring and genuinely concerned about his well-being; then on the other hand, I was manipulative, arrogant, and sometimes downright nasty toward him. At one point, I provoked him into slapping me because I wanted to know how it felt to be slapped by a boyfriend. I drew him out of his character with my character flaws and hang-ups that were rooted in the events that took place early on in my life. I didn't know how to receive anything good because I had a twisted perception of what good was. I didn't think I was happy unless drama was surrounding my life and I was the victim.

Although Chris was the ideal boyfriend, I broke up with him to start dating Orlando, the not-so-ideal boyfriend. I could not appreciate the pure honest love that Chris showed me but I ate up the drama and heartache that Orlando gave me. I met Orlando in downtown Chicago (what is it with me and meeting men in downtown Chicago). I was still dating Chris but did not think twice about cheating on him and dating Orlando.

Orlando and Chris were like night and day. Chris was honest and straight forward while Orlando was a liar and sneaky. My mother hated Orlando on sight and could not understand what I saw in him. She saw right through him, while all I saw was a cute face. Orlando was a cocaine user, a liar, a drinker, and an all-around bad guy but I clung to him and tried to make it work. Even though I had caught him in several lies, I still acted if I was clueless. I held on to him because I did not think that I could get better or deserved better. I gave up better when I gave up Chris, but I gravitated toward the struggle of trying to get better out of Orlando. This is the type of mentality that I had when it came to men and relationships. I did not know how to receive anything that would uplift me but instead I gravitated toward everything that caused me pain. I was not happy unless I was in a drama induced struggle.

After my high school graduation, at the age of eighteen, I enlisted in the U.S. Navy and found myself away from home and living on my own for the first time. After boot camp, my first duty station was Bermuda. Needless to say it was a whole new world for me and quite the experience. One of the greatest things that being in the military taught me was the ability to take care of myself, that was an easy lesson to learn. But because I was ill equipped mentally and emotionally to engage in healthy relationships, I developed a cycle of allowing the wrong people to be in my life.

Even though I had left Chicago to begin a new life, I took the old me with me. The insecurity, low self-esteem, rejection, abandonment, and anger issues that I dealt with at home were the same issues that I carried with me. I still viewed myself in a low state and it reflected greatly in the decisions that I made when it came to dating.

While in Bermuda, I never had a problem getting a man. There were times when I had a "pair and a spare." The problem lay in the type of men that I dated and the craziness that I would subject myself to. I was always a sucker for a good looking man and when he found me attractive I did whatever I needed to do to keep his attention.

At times I was a walking contradiction. I would put up a front of being strong and that nothing bothered me, when deep down inside the rejection of a lost love secretly destroyed me. Still having a warped sense of what love was and having no real self-worth, I traded the good for the bad. This happened when I started dating this guy named Harry.

Harry was a cute light-skinned Bermudian with beautiful green eyes. We met at this popular nightclub called Touch which was located in the Princess Anne Hotel. I was there with some co-workers and he was there with his friends. We spotted each other across the floor and before the night was over had exchanged numbers. We started dating and after a few months, he moved in with me. For a while things were fine and I convinced myself that I was happy. I completely overlooked his immaturity and his inability to give me what I needed emotionally just to be with him. Harry was not a bad guy but had I been in a place where I loved myself, I would have rethought the relationship.

Things began to get really bad and came to an end when he saw me give a guy a ride up the hill on my scooter. He accused me of being unfaithful but I think he was just looking for a way out. I remember having an argument with him that night when I got home. In the heat of the discussion I found myself saying to him, "Oh, so I'm a hoe and no good," and he agreed. I can't believe those words came out of my mouth referring to myself and what hurt me the most is that he had the nerve to agree. In that moment I snapped and told him to just get out if he felt that way about me. He did not leave that night but the reality of loneliness hit when I came home from work the next night and found him packing his bags and loading them into his friend's car. I was distraught and physically ill that night. For weeks I mourned a love that did not love me in return and would have taken him back at any given moment. At that time, I could not see that it was only an imitation of love because I did not know what real love was.

In the process of trying to get over Harry I met and started to date this really nice guy named Simone. Simone was from England and had a beautiful accent. He had piercing blue eyes and blond hair. He was a policeman and he liked me very much. He was another keeper that I did not want to keep. He was good to me and drama free, but I was bad for him. I knew that he liked me so I played mind games with him, toying with his emotions. Since Simone was not one for playing games, although he liked me, he did not want to deal with me. To make matters worse, I found myself back with Harry. We were back together long enough to sleep together. It all ended one night when I met him at the club.

When Harry and I got back together it was not what I thought it would be. We weren't together long before he started acting funny. Once again I went into my "do all you can to keep him because you don't want to be alone" mode. On the night that it all fell apart we had made plans to meet at the club that evening. I found that strange because he would always come and pick me up. When I arrived at the club, Harry had not yet arrived. I sat down and sitting across from me was this pretty fair skinned girl with long black hair talking to her friends about this guy. As Harry walked through the door, the pretty, fair skinned girl with the long black hair became really excited and said, "There he is."

Needless to say when she said that and looked his way, I got angry. Harry and I had been fighting earlier because I had noticed a hickey on his neck. Of course he denied everything but judging from the way this girl reacted to him walking in, he was about to get caught in a lie. I walked up to him and asked him who she was. He claimed that she was just a friend and part of the wedding party that he had participated in that day. I knew it was a lie but I so wanted to give him the benefit of the doubt. My intellect was telling me that he wasn't being completely honest and that I should cut my losses, maintain my dignity and go, but I didn't. I wanted to believe him, and I dreaded the thought that I may be alone.

The soul wounds kept me from striving for anything outside of pain. It all came to a climax when he totally disrespected me and asked her to dance while I was sitting right there. I felt as if he had slapped me in my face. When he got off the dance floor, he sat down and the girl sat next to him. I don't think she knew that I was his girlfriend until she briefly looked my way and saw the contempt in my eyes as I glared at her. I asked Harry if I could speak to him for a moment. I asked him what was going on and without even flinching he told me that it was over and left me standing there as he walked away to be with her. I was embarrassed and humiliated. That incident took me back to my high school days when the boys would choose the pretty light complexion girls with the long hair over me. The girl that Harry chose over me was a beautiful Spanish girl with long flowing hair. As I walked up the stairs to leave the club I realized that once again rejection slapped me in the face.

That night his best friend took me home. My first thought was to sleep with his best friend as a way of retaliation and I could have, but I didn't. Even after all of that, for a while, I was still drawn to Harry. Once again my fragmented soul kept me from a relationship that would have been good for me and drew me into a relationship that was emotionally destructive. Even though I'd had a nice guy, Simone, who treated me well, because I was operating out of an emotional wounded place, I gravitated toward the hurt that Harry offered. At one point I tried to go back to Simone but he'd moved on and didn't have time for the games that I played. I really couldn't blame him because he did not want his emotions toyed with. I saw him one day with a beautiful young lady and he looked happy. I just looked and regretted that it wasn't me.

I eventually got over Harry and started dating an older gentleman, Kendal. Kendal was from Trinidad and he worked at the Navy Exchange. He was a good guy but like older guys who date younger women, he always tried to "teach" me something. I was only dating him in the beginning because he would shower me with gifts and he would make me clothes. I knew that I was not serious about him and as soon as we got engaged, I was thinking of ways to get out of it. I can't say that I really cared for Kendal as much as he did for me. In fact, the more that I think about it, he was just something for me to do. Once again, I was toying with and manipulating someone else's emotions. I needed to control everything and I needed this control because for so long I had no control. Little did I know that I was about to lose control and experience the love of my life.

My relationship with Kendal was a vehicle that God used to bring me to salvation. Kendal stayed with his mother and every time I would go to his house his mom would call me into her bedroom to witness to me and read the Bible to me. I did not like it but I could not say no to his mother. The turning point was when she invited me to church and I said yes. I said yes because I really wanted her to stop inviting me. I even had Kendal make me a dress to let her know that I was serious about going.

That Sunday when I went to church, the evangelist administering the Word asked if there was anyone in the building that needed Christ. All I remember was when I came to myself, I was at the altar. It was as if my spirit walked to the altar and my body caught up to it. As I stood in front of the evangelist and Pastor Tuzo, I realized that my life was about to change. That was the day that I received Jesus Christ as my Savior.

When I transferred to Norfolk, Virginia, once again I was facing a whole new world. Although I had received Christ as my Savior, I was still dealing with the same issues. I needed to be delivered and healed from the wounds that had been inflicted on me as a child that I had carried into my adulthood. I still had the need to be accepted and found myself in situations that I shouldn't have been in just to keep friends. I was timid, did not know how to stand up for myself, and was angry because I couldn't. Even though I was professing Christ, the company that I kept did not allow me to be a good follower of Christ.

I started dating this young man named James. James was half black, half Pilipino. He was fine but he was not nice. He was unfaithful and had the tendency to be verbally abusive, but I held on to him with everything I had - sound familiar? I recall one night we got into an argument and I literally begged him not to leave me. How sad a state I was in. Here I was begging a man to stay with me for fear of being alone. How much was I to take before I got the picture that I did not have to indulge in these life-draining relationships? That relationship ended when I met my first husband, Carlos.

Carlos and I married young. I was 24 and he was 22. He was a Marine and I met him one night while my girlfriend and I were out on the town. We dated for about a year and then we married. For Carlos to be so young, he was a good husband. He was very family- oriented and was excited about being a husband and one day a father. I knew that Carlos loved me because he was the type of man that did not toy with emotions. I confided in him about the things that went on in my childhood and his heart went out to me. He tried to be the best husband that he could but I still couldn't love him the way I needed to. I was incapable of loving from a pure place so I loved him from a wounded place. That love was unhealthy and it demanded much more then it was capable of giving; something that he could not provide.

I was still in a place where I had to control everything including the intimacy. I rejected him in so many ways in fear of his rejection. I did not know how to love him. Although it had been many years since the incestuous relationship between my uncle and I, the soul tie was still very much alive. Not that I wanted to be with my uncle, as a matter of fact, I hated my uncle, but because the bond had never been cut, our souls were still knit together from the relations that we had. This was evident during the times I was intimate with my husband. I never understood why he had to touch me a certain way in order for me to respond to him. I would find myself positioning my body to be in the same position that it would be in when I sat on my uncle's lap when he fondled me. That was the only position I could receive

Carlos' touch. There were also times when he could not just come up to me and touch me because I would get very defensive. It would take me back to when my uncle grabbed and squeezed my bottom or just came up to me to pull up my shirt. The battle that I was experiencing in my soul prevented me from being able to fully give myself to my husband. I was so very flawed that I was unable to relinquish any kind of control when it came to intimacy, even though that intimacy was with my husband.

Our marriage ended in four years. The last year that we were together was difficult for both of us. I had pushed him away one too many times and he was fed up. During that period, I went into victim–mode and tried everything to change his mind. When I found that my tactics didn't work, I would put up this façade and pretend that I didn't care. When he left me I suffered the biggest bout with depression that I had ever suffered.

Our breakup came during a time I was recovering from an illness. The medication I was on caused me to gain weight, and I was very unattractive to myself. I had been discharged from the military and my life was changing drastically. When Carlos walked out on me, I was left shattered and broken. He moved back to New Orleans and never looked back. His actions reinforced the rejection and the abandonment issues that I was already dealing with. For months I lay on my couch unable to function outside of getting up daily and going to work. Depression and the psychic hotline had become my friends. I was going to church but no one knew the agony I was in. I had no one to talk to so I started talking to the people on the physic hotline. I remember calling the psychic hotline one day and the lady on the line said something to me that shook me back into some sense of reality. The words that this "psychic" spoke to me were "You need to pray to God." At that moment I knew that God was speaking.

I managed to pull myself together and get over my husband and once again, instead of dealing with my emotions, I suppressed them. I threw away or burned everything that he gave me and I pretended our marriage never existed. That was my way of coping and staying in denial about the deep hurt. I figured if I said I did not care enough, I would eventually not care. Even when Carlos and I spoke I put up a front and told him what a mistake I'd made when I married him. I wanted to hurt him for hurting me, so every chance I got, I reminded him of my big mistake of being with him.

After Carlos, there were other relationships that I indulged in, but none ever brought the fulfillment that I needed. Since I was in a place of brokenness, I chose the men that would break me even more. I chose men that were broken and I thought that I could fix them. So I self-sacrificed and instead of knowing my worth, I downgraded my value and chose to be with those who had nothing to offer.

In 1999 I met Vincent Jacobs, my second husband, through a friend of mine. At the time that I met Vincent, I had been divorced for five years and I was ready to be married again, or so I thought. I was still in a place that I needed to be accepted and with that need comes certain desperation.

Vincent and I married six months after we met and that was a mistake. There are always signs of someone's character that are often shown but it is up to us to recognize those signs. Vincent had problems with his mom and that should have been a red flag that I should not have ignored. It wasn't that he didn't love his mother but it seemed that they had unresolved issues. Vincent turned out to be emotionally abusive. He always complained about my weight, which caused me to spiral deeper into the abyss of low self-esteem. He did not know how to speak to me and would often take a tone that left me feeling that I was not good enough for him. Vincent had demons he was fighting as well. He was in no more of an emotional position to be married than I was. I realized how emotionally torn we both were when one argument turned into a physical altercation.

I'd had choir rehearsal one night that went on longer than anticipated. I did not get home until midnight. Something told me that I should have called, but I did not. When I got home I found a note on the table stating that he went out to look for me. That same voice, the voice of the Lord, who told me to call, told me to start praying. Once again, I ignored that voice. When Vincent came in the door he was very upset. I tried to explain to him that I was at choir rehearsal but he didn't want to hear it. He said that he was worried about me and could literally smell my hair. He said that he had gone out to look for me because he thought that something had happened.

I followed him into the room still trying to speak with him and he abruptly said "Why are you jockin' me?" I said, "What?" He began to go off on me cursing and talking down to me. The next thing I knew I blanked out and physically jumped on him. When I came to myself my fingernails were embedded in his neck and I saw blood streaming down. He grabbed me and as he did that I tripped and fell backward hitting my head on the dresser. As I scrambled to get up I realized that I had also twisted my ankle. He began to pack his clothes and I tried to convince him to stop so we could talk about it. He was angry and still talking down to me. He said that I was just like my mother, Geraldine.

What I said next not only shocked me but it scared him. I told him that if I were like my mother, I would have gotten a knife and stabbed him thirteen times. In that moment, as he stood there looking at me, I knew that I was messed up. To think about stabbing him was a major disruption in my way of thinking, but I was angry enough to have considered it. I left the house and went to sit on the stairs of our apartment building. As I cried, I tried to figure out what was wrong with me and why was love so hard.

We got through that night but our marriage didn't last long. Vincent got a job that required travel and the more he traveled the more he hated to come home. The more he came home, the more I wanted him to leave. I did not trust him with my heart and he had issues within himself that he needed to deal with.

I remember when our marriage was on the brink of ending the Lord had given me a dream. In that dream Vincent and I were on the beach and it was filled with women. He was walking around talking to every woman on the beach and completely ignoring me. In the dream I pulled him aside and asked him what was going on and he said that he did not want to be with me anymore.

I shared this dream with my spiritual aunt and she told me what that dream meant. As a matter of fact, she told me everything that was going on in the marriage. My husband traveled with his job a lot and was in a position to meet a lot of people. The Lord was telling me that my husband had emotionally disconnected from the marriage and it would not be long before he would walk out of the marriage. My aunt said that by the end of the year he would be gone and I would not have to pay for the divorce but after the divorce I could not date anyone. I would have to allow the Lord to heal me from all the hurt and pain. This was in October when she revealed this to me. By December my husband had moved out and by the spring of the following year we were divorced. Once again I was left rejected and abandoned. This union lasted a little over a year.

At the end of that marriage I was emotionally spent. I tried to cover up my true feelings by dating other men, which only resulted in more rejection. I sank deeper and deeper into depression. Even though

I was in church, I had no one to really speak to regarding these issues I was having. I even found myself going to a psychiatrist to see if I could be released from the turmoil that I was going through. During the sessions with the psychiatrist we discovered that the root of everything was due to the relationship that I'd had with my uncle but it did not give me any insight on how to be delivered from the demons that I dealt with because of the relationship. This type of release required more than me talking about my problems. I was involved in spiritual warfare and was ill equipped to fight.

There were many random relationships that left me empty. I wanted to be loved but just did not know how to be. I didn't even love myself so how could I give what I didn't have. I had two broken marriages and a few broken relationships that left me emotionally desolate. I didn't know what to do with myself or how to cope. There were times that I literally wanted to scream, rant and rave and then there were those times when I just wanted to lie down and sleep my life away.

The relationships that I just described are the woes of someone who has been sexually abused and trying to be loved when I didn't know what real love was. The ability to know what pure love is had been taken from me. All I had left was the aftermath of the sexual assault. All I had left was a war that was going on in my soul and I was losing. The stigma of my past was tattooed on my soul.

CHAPTER 8

What's Hurting Me?

Last night I found myself watching Tyler Perry's movie, "I Can Do Bad All By Myself." I have seen this movie several times but this particular time I was looking at it with new eyes. This time I was fully able to relate to April's character. April puts on this hard-core, nothing-affects-me persona when, deep down, she is confused and hurting. This hurt is evident in the life that she lived. She's a heavy drinker who finds solace in sleeping with a married man. She rejects her niece and nephews even though she is their last hope. When a good man came into her life and showed a genuine interest, she rejected him just to hang on to the married man who had nothing to offer but sex and a wife with five kids. The truth of her deep seated woes come to light when her boyfriend attacks her sixteen- year-old niece. He denies the attack and actually accuses the niece of trying to seduce him. This incident enrages April because it takes her back to when she was raped as a child by her uncle and was blamed for the incident.

April never had the opportunity to heal from the rape that she endured as a young girl and the devastation of her mother not believing her. Not only was her innocence snatched from her but she was left to shoulder the crime that was against her. The brokenness she buried deep within her manifested through her inability to give love as well as to receive love. This was demonstrated when she rejected her niece and nephews when they needed her the most. She did not have the ability to give them the love and acceptance that they so desperately needed because she was numb to the fact that she needed that very same love and acceptance. April deemed herself unworthy because she limited herself to an unfulfilling affair that she was having with the married man. Her hurt was so deep that she walked in denial of her pain and masked it with bad decisions, alcohol, and a "I-don't-care-about-anything-or-anyone" attitude.

Sexual abuse is especially devastating to a child because it confuses both their mind and emotions. One does not walk out of this trauma without mental and emotional battle scars that are designed to manipulate and distort one's view of what love is. Below are some reasons why this kind of assault is so crushing and how adults suffer from unresolved childhood wounds.

Betrayal:

Sexual abuse, especially to a child, is distressing because it often comes from a loved one that they trust and look to as a protector. The abuse shatters the closeness of the relationship because the abuser has turned that pure bond into a selfish, self-gratifying, sexual act. The moment that line is crossed, in a child's mind, the protector has now become the predator and the feeling of safety is shattered. Every time the child hears the abuser's name or comes into direct contact with him or her, that child is reminded of the hurt and pain. Any healthy memories of the relationship have now been overshadowed by the horror of the offense. This betrayal opens the door for the child to have trust issues.

Confusion:

God created sex as a beautiful expression of love shared between a man and a woman in the sanctity of marriage. This is a gift of intimacy and pleasure designed to bring a husband and wife closer together. When one uses their relationship, such as that between an uncle and a niece, to gain sex, it is for selfish reasons and not for love. This will confuse the abused because they may learn to associate love with selfishness. The abuser has taken an act that should be associated with tenderness and understanding, designed specifically to be received from one's spouse, and polluted it to serve their own perverted desires. This will ultimately make the abused feel like an object that has been used and discarded. This perplexes the abused and they often have trouble distinguishing between love and selfishness in future relationships. Once the abused has been used for the selfish pleasure of someone else, their perception of what is a healthy love and what is an unhealthy imitation of love has been tainted. This misperception of what is healthy love and what is unhealthy makes it difficult for the abused one to receive true, authentic, pure love in the future; so they often settle for a counterfeit love.

Negative Feelings Associated with Closeness:

An uncle to niece relationship should be similar to a father to daughter relationship. A healthy relationship between them should be founded on and deeply rooted in trust, security, protection, kindness, acceptance and joy. This is also true for a husband and wife engaged in a sexual relationship but at a much deeper level. When the lines become blurred and boundaries are crossed because of abuse, that action strips the abused of the trust, security, protection and kindness that they had with that person. That healthy covering is no longer there and the abused, in a sense, becomes exposed and naked which causes them to experience feelings of guilt, shame, exploitation, condemnation, fear, rejection, anger, and loss. These negative emotions are often taken into future relationships.

Many victims of abuse are so ashamed of what took place that they attempt to blot out every memory of the abuse and suppress what happened. This may work for a while but very often something will occur that will open the door to those suppressed memories and emotions. Unfortunately, when that happens anger is often the emotion that comes to the forefront and an unsuspecting friend, spouse or child will be the bear the brunt of those negative feelings and hurtful actions. This eruption may cause the abused person to feel guilty and they are left in an uncomfortable place wondering where all of that anger came from. He or she is ashamed of the attack and begins to feel bad about themselves for being the cause of it. They are constantly wondering why they did it and will often condemn themselves which only intensifies the negative image they already hold of themselves. These abrupt bouts of anger and withdrawal confirm that they have associated negative feelings with closeness and their denial has only further delayed their healing.

Change:

When a child is a victim of sexual abuse a drastic change takes place internally. They have been stripped of their innocence and often feel degraded and cheap. What was meant to be a gift to a future husband or wife has now become a stolen, forbidden fruit given unwillingly to someone else. This leaves them with feelings of worthlessness and often they see themselves as damaged, devalued, and unworthy of anything good. They face future relationships with the fear of being used and then tossed aside.

Building Emotional Barriers:

Often, those who suffer from abuse have a tendency to build up emotional barriers (obstacles). A barrier is simply something that prevents or blocks movement from one place to another. They build these barriers because of a lack of trust and in fear of being hurt again. These barriers serve as a protective mechanism that won't allow anyone to penetrate the heart and emotions of the abused. The abused is usually uncomfortable with anyone getting to close to them because at an early age experience had taught them that "loved ones" are not to be trusted and that you can't depend on them to keep you safe and secure. This blockage prevents anyone from getting in close and it prevents the abused from being able to receive or give emotionally. This can lead to a very lonely life for the abused because of their inability to build intimate and close relationships.

Inability to Receive Love:

The victim of abuse may have an inability to receive love even when it's genuine and coming from a good and healthy place. They often feel unworthy and undeserving and associate love with the pain of abuse. Even when in a genuinely loving relationship, it is hard for the abused to erase the memories of the trespass and wholeheartedly embrace a partner who is loving and supportive. In my case, I wanted to be loved but when it was presented to me I rejected it because I did not trust it. I did not know what a healthy love looked or felt like. Even when I allowed myself to receive something that was good, I found a way to sabotage it because I felt that it was too good to be true and that, eventually, I would be hurt. It seems that I was not happy unless I was miserable. I gave and I received love from a broken place which perpetuated the indulgence in a cycle of relationships that only prolonged and magnified my feeling of worthlessness.

A Need to Control:

Victims of abuse often deal with the need to control. Webster defines control as "to have power over." This becomes important to the victim because when the abuse was taking place all control was taken away from them. They had no voice in the matter of what took place and they were stripped of their security to feel safe. Their power over their physical body and their human rights - to not to be sexually assaulted – had been taken away. They take on the mentality that "no one will ever have control over me again." Often, along with this need to control, certain demands are placed on friends and loved ones. If we are not careful, the need to control can turn into an act of manipulation. What the victim does not realize is that God is the only one who can offer security, restore our body, and re-establish our rights.

Insecurity, Low Self Esteem and a Need for Acceptance:

Victims of abuse often struggle with insecurity and low self-esteem. This was something that I struggled with greatly. Confidence in self or the ability to do anything right became an overwhelming task. My insecurity walked hand-in-hand with low self-esteem and it was reflected in the men I dated, the jobs I took and the friends I chose. Because of my fear and low self-esteem, I became a people-pleaser and often presented myself as a target to be taken advantage of. When I was taken advantage of, that further reinforced the feelings of rejection and worthlessness that I felt.

Anger:

Anger is one of the biggest issues that an abused person will deal with. For me, that anger was deeply seated and explosive. My anger issues started before I was sexually abused. The seed of anger was planted when I saw my mother, Geraldine, getting beaten by her boyfriend and it was further reinforced by my abrupt separation from my mother and my sister. The sexual abuse only intensified that emotion. I remember as a teenager there were times when I would get so angry that I would destroy my room by throwing things around. It was uncontrollable. My anger also manifested when I was babysitting my four-year-old cousin and I disciplined him severely, leaving bruises on his face and wrist from me tying him up. My heart breaks even now as I think about the physical pain that I caused him as a child; however, I have had the opportunity as an adult to repent to him and receive his forgiveness.

This anger stayed with me as an adult. I could not figure out why I had these uncontrollable outbursts and couldn't seem to let things go. I soon discovered that this anger was rooted in all that I had experienced as a child. My anger would not begin to settle until I began to walk in true forgiveness. I had to forgive my uncle for the sexual abuse. I had to forgive Geraldine for the emotional abuse. I had to forgive everyone else who hurt me - including myself.

This is what I was dealing with. I had bouts of rage and excessive control issues, when, in fact, I was out of control. My inability to give myself completely to those that chose to love me was instrumental in the demise of my first marriage. I was emotionally depleted. Even though I had received Christ and was doing the best I could with what I knew (which wasn't much), I was still empty, broken and in denial.

After years of warring with my emotions and fighting this battle with the wrong tools, I finally decided that only God could help me. I had been living for him but I had not relinquished that part of my life to him. I kept those feelings locked deep inside and did not trust God enough to be able to wash away the guilt and shame and to heal me from the past pain. Because I had no idea of what pure love was, I could not receive God's perfect love because to me, his love was the same love that I had been experiencing all along - a love that was broken, selfish and unfulfilling. But even in the midst of that wrong thinking, I knew that there had to be something better and that I had to strive to achieve wholeness.

I knew that I had a long journey ahead of me and that the journey would not be easy because it would require me to come to terms with some things and reveal the tattered little girl who had suffered in silence for so many years. It was time to release the little girl who was buried deep inside me. Not only did it require the tattered little girl to be exposed, it required her to come to terms with some harsh realities and ultimately forgive herself and those who violated her.

CHAPTER 9

I Forgive Him, I Forgive Him NOT!
(He Can Go to HELL as Far as I am Concerned)

The Bible tells us that if we do not forgive, the Father will not forgive us. There is no getting around it. The scriptures leave no room for unforgiveness. Matthew 6:15 states *"But if ye forgive not men their trespasses, neither will your Father forgive your trespasses."* The Bible goes on to tell us in Matthew 5:7 *"Blessed are the merciful, for they will be shown mercy."* Not only that, but God has the audacity, so we think, to tell us in Matthew 5:44 that we have to love our enemies, do good to those that curse you, and to pray for them who spitefully use you. As you see, God is very clear that forgiveness is not an option for those of us who want to remain in right standing with him. The truth is, we have to forgive in order to be forgiven, but it is much more than that. We have to forgive if we want to be set free, if we want to be healed, and if we want to walk in deliverance.

The concept of forgiveness sounds all fine and dandy and when you read these scriptures your spirit bears witness to the truth of them. At a certain level you honestly receive what the Word is saying and you take sincere steps toward applying that Word to your heart and circumstance. The challenge of forgiveness comes when your soul reminds you of the abuse and the pain that you're still suffering as the tattered little girl within you, who never received her healing as a child, begins to cry. She begins to speak out loud about the times her abuser's hand fondled and squeezed her breast while the fingers from the other hand probed and crammed their way up her vagina. The child within still feels the shame and can't shake the feeling of being a worthless whore. Every time she cries in anguish and frustration, the spirits of anger, bitterness, and hate settle deeper into her soul and suddenly forgiveness becomes a foreign word and an obsolete concept.

The pain endured from a trespass can be so great that we cannot walk in the very thing that will begin our journey to healing and that is forgiveness. Sadly, there are many men and women who harbor unforgiveness toward their abuser and never receive the deliverance and freedom that they desperately need.

Satan uses unforgiveness as a tool to manipulate. He knows that unforgiveness will cut us off from fully accessing God; and if we are not accessing God, we are vulnerable to Satan's attacks. Satan convinces us, through the pain, to hold on to unforgiveness. Holding on to unforgiveness gives us this twisted notion that we are somehow getting back at the person who hurt us. Once again, Satan has lied to you for that is the furthest thing from the truth. The person that you are holding on to through bitterness and hatred most likely has moved on with their life, while you are still bound and in turmoil. Forgiving that person has nothing to do with that person. You are not letting them off the hook. On the contrary, forgiveness is to break the chains and to release you from the bondage of that circumstance.

When we choose not to forgive, we are choosing to stay in agreement with the hurt. We make a covenant with the trespass and we keep it alive in our emotions and in our thoughts. Satan knows this so he keeps us bound with anger, bitterness, condemnation and shame. These are spirits that gain legal access from the trauma of the trespass. If we walk hand-in-hand with these spirits, any attempt of true deliverance will be in vain.

During this journey, I had to learn what true forgiveness really was and what it looked like. I had to come to the realization that Jesus was not going to open up the heavens and release a beam of light upon me so that I would suddenly have this flourishing heart of forgiveness. No, God does not work like that; it would be nice if He did, but He doesn't. We are left with the task of participating in our deliverance. He tells us in his Word that we have a choice between life and death and that choice is left up to us. My choice was to either forgive and allow God to do work within me; or I could wallow in self-pity and never really achieve the full deliverance that my Father wanted for me.

Even though I knew the seriousness of forgiveness and believed everything that the Word said about it, true forgiveness was not in my vocabulary for a very long time. Although my uncle, on many occasions, had apologized, I did not trust that he was sincere. I hated the fact that he had moved on and was living a seemingly good life. I hated that he felt no remorse or that God had not punished him for what he had done. I hated everything about him and his ability to live as if nothing happened. I wanted him to suffer as I had for all those years. Instead, he had gotten married and had children and interacted with other children. I often asked myself "How could this be?" And the more I thought about it, the angrier I got. The angrier I got, the more I closed the door to forgiveness and kept my uncle locked up in my mental jail cell with no chance of a pardon or parole. With all of these emotions hidden, yet brewing inside, I still allowed the devil to convince me that I had forgiven. There were even been times when I told my uncle that I forgave him while secretly damning him to hell.

This journey toward true forgiveness did not actually begin until 2010. There were times when I said that I had forgiven but had not. I sincerely wanted to forgive but I just did not know how. I reasoned with myself and believed that since I was not verbally damning him to hell or thinking about him with disdain, I was okay. But I wasn't okay. I was lying to myself and walking in false forgiveness.

False forgiveness will allow you to think that you have forgiven a person but in reality you are just masking the pain and harboring hate and disdain. False forgiveness blocks the Master Surgeon's (Jesus Christ's) hands from cleansing the emotional wounds of bitterness and hurt. This deception tells you that you are all right while you secretly deal with bouts of anger and contempt. Every time something occurs that triggers a memory or the sight of that person or the sound of their name, it leaves you physically ill. I had a form of forgiveness while rejecting the power of true forgiveness

I was denying that I was still in great pain and I needed more than just a quick fix at the altar to release the little abused child that was deep inside me. I came to the realization that no matter how many times I went to the altar and cried, hollered, and did whatever I thought I had to do to be set free, I was still bound. No matter how many sessions I had with my psychiatrist, I was still bound. The wounds were still open and the infection of bitterness had set in. If not dealt with, the poison of bitterness would, in the end, kill me spiritually. I needed a healing beyond my own strength.

God began to deal with me about forgiving my uncle through prayer. I would begin to pray and the Lord would place my uncle's face right in front of me. The first time the Lord presented my uncle to me in prayer, my reaction was not too favorable and I was blatantly rebellious. I can remember saying to the Lord "I am not praying for him. He can go to hell as far as I'm concerned." Can you imagine the nerve that I had speaking to the Holy Ghost that way? I said it out loud and I distinctly remember the hardening of my heart and the venom in my voice when I said it. I can recall the anger I felt. I could not comprehend why God would want me to pray for someone who, on countless occasions, used my body and stripped me of my self-worth. But, as angry as I was, I recognized that my heart was hardened and that all those times that I had confessed forgiveness were just mere words uttered without conviction. I was not at a place spiritually to comprehend that through my un-forgiveness I was unknowingly keeping the door open for the enemy to condemn me and keep me in bondage. Through unforgiveness I was giving the devil legal access to my emotions. I was keeping the trespass alive and slamming the door in the face of true deliverance. The enemy had placed a chain around my neck and every time I went to leap into my destiny, he would yank me back. In a way, I had tied God's hands because through my actions, I had given the devil permission to invade my life.

The more I resisted praying for him, the more the Lord placed him before me. Finally, I started praying generic prayers. These prayers didn't have any substance and they were not heartfelt. Actually, my prayers were self-centered. I really was not concerned about him repenting so that he could receive salvation. I cared more about God humbling him so he could repent for what he had done to me. I was trying to manipulate God into passing judgment while God was trying to get me to a place of breakthrough. Needless to say, God was not receiving any of these prayers.

One day, during prayer, I found myself praying earnestly for my uncle. I can recall asking God to truly save him. From that prayer on, I started redirecting my words. I started declaring out loud that I forgave him for all that he had done to me.

Every day I would say, "I forgive my uncle" for such and such and such. I literally called out each offense and declared forgiveness. This type of declaration began to change my heart. I declared forgiveness for him; I declared forgiveness for myself and the part that I played in the incestuous relationship. I began to look at him differently. He went from an abuser to a soul that needed salvation.

I was constantly hearing teachings on forgiveness and one lesson led me to ponder what could possibly have made him do what he did. What would make an uncle want to engage in sexual relations, of any sort, with his niece? Wasn't an uncle's role to protect and be a second father to a child? Blood relative or not, we are family. Did other families work like this? How did he become a conduit of that perverse spirit? What had made him sick, for only sick people have the ability to contaminate and make others sick. He was dealing with perverse spirits unaware. Had this spirit been in the generation of men in his family and was it just being filtered down? That question was easily answered as a hidden memory resurfaced of my grandfather, my uncle's father.

My brother and I were waiting on the corner of Belmont and Clark. I was told that my grandfather was going to pick us up and to be on the lookout for him. As my grandfather pulled up, we jumped in the backseat of the car. My grandfather turned around and begin to speak to me and as he was speaking to me he reached over the front seat and used his right index finger to brush up and down on my right breast.

He stopped talking and looked at me and all I could do was drop my head. I never told anyone, not even my uncle. That was the role model and the influence that my uncle grew up under. The perverse spirit was clearly a transference from father to son, from one generation to the next.

As the Word of God on forgiveness began to take root in me, I began to let go of the rage. I no longer wanted it nor did I have the strength to bear the weight of the sins of the past. There was no energy left to hold on to the grudge and I was tired of attending my own pity party. Was it tragic what I experienced? Yes, it was. No child should ever experience this sort of relationship with a relative or any adult for that matter. But it was time to unlock the chains that had me shackled and to release this offense from my mental jail cell.

My confession of forgiveness was put to the test in 2010. I had completed my year of training for Eagles International Training Institute and I was excitedly getting ready for my graduation that was to take place in Texas. My very best friend, who is also named Kim, was coming and I was so thrilled to be completing this great accomplishment. I was in a new place spiritually and I really felt that I was on my way to greater things.

My uncle lived in Texas at that time, which really was no big deal to me considering I had no plans to see him while I was there. I was still confessing my forgiveness and God was healing me but I was not quite ready to see him face-to-face. Well, God's plans are not our plans. The Holy Spirit spoke to me and told me to invite him to my graduation. Remember, I had been claiming forgiveness for about a year and the time had come for me to walk in what I had been professing. When the Holy Ghost told me to invite my uncle to my graduation, I had mixed feelings. I knew that this was a turning point for me. I called my dear friend Kim and discussed it with her. Kim was well aware of the situation, for she knew about the abuse that had taken place. She said that it was time to release the hurt and all that came with it and move forward.

I really didn't know how the initial phone call to my uncle would go. The times before when I had spoken to my uncle, which were not many, it was usually me answering my mom's phone. Even then, when I heard his voice I became very cold and usually rushed to transfer him to the party that he needed to speak to. When he picked up the phone, I detected the surprise in his voice. I told him that I would be in Texas for my Eagles graduation and that I would like for him to attend. I could hear relief in his voice as if he was saying finally we can put the past behind us. He told me that he would love to attend and would if his schedule permitted. I really didn't know how I felt about that because if he did come, I would have to walk in what I'd been professing. This encounter was going to let me know if I had truly forgiven him or if I was just walking around once again giving lip service to the Lord. I must admit I struggled with it for awhile. Had the Holy Ghost not prompted me to invite him, I wouldn't have done so. God has a way of allowing situations to manifest so that you can see where you really are in Him.

My uncle was unable to come to the graduation and I can't say that I didn't feel a little relieved. But God was not through working with me. I wasn't getting off the hook that easily. This was a test to see if I had really released him from his trespass. Although he was unable to come to the graduation, he didn't want to miss the opportunity to see me. We decided that Kim and I would go out to lunch with him.

I didn't know how I felt about meeting him in such an intimate gathering. It would have been much easier for me if he had just come to the graduation. The room full of people and the limited time we would've had to communicate would have been just the safety net I needed to avoid anything that may still be rooted. Now I was faced with having to go to lunch with him and his wife, not really knowing what emotions would erupt. I kept thinking about how I would react when I saw his face. I kept wondering if his wife knew the situation and if she did, what did she really know. A lot of things ran through my mind and I really started to question whether or not I had truly forgiven him.

When he arrived at the hotel to pick us up, I did not feel the anxiety that I thought I would when I came face-to-face with him. During the ride to the restaurant and in between the small talk, I tried to muster up any type of derogatory feelings that I thought I should have for him. We went to this Tex-

Mex restaurant and I was seated right next to him. I remember frequently glancing at him while trying to conjure up every memory of everything that he had ever done to me so that I could muster up just an inkling of hate; but my mind was blank. At that moment in time, I wanted to remember so that I could accuse him. I wanted a reason to hate him and to expose all that he had done but I couldn't. There was no hate to conjure up and there were no feelings of animosity. At that point in time, I thought, maybe forgiveness was obtainable. Maybe if I just let go and release him, we both can heal.

After lunch, he drove us back to the hotel. Before we got out of the car I found myself asking them if I could pray. I prayed and it was well received. As we parted, I felt such a heaviness leaving me. I knew right then and there, that I could move on from the past. As I thought about it, there had been many times when my uncle had apologized for sexually abusing me. The times that he had apologized I had been unable to receive it because I was driven by the hurt and the hate. Not only that, I hadn't forgiven myself. The shame of my participation kept me locked in a place where I could not rise above it or move forward. It was easy for me to blame someone else for my misery but I had to honestly ask myself how great of a participant was I in the madness? My eyes had to be open to the fact that I had to repent and receive God's forgiveness for myself and then I had to forgive myself. What a wonderful release that was to finally come into knowing that forgiveness and letting go was the refreshment that my soul needed.

As I settled myself that night, I had found new found hope. I knew that with this new-found freedom the healing process would begin. I was ready to allow the tattered little girl to receive the healing that would allow the adult woman to move forward. I knew that I was to face a journey ahead for there was much my soul needed to be released from, but I had made the first step in claiming my freedom. I had made my first commitment to cooperating with my deliverance process; I was on my way to recovery.

CHAPTER 10

Recovery
(The Process of Healing)

Forgiveness is the very thing that propelled me on my journey to recovery. Forgiveness was the opening God needed in order to heal my broken and fragmented soul. God is our potter and we are like clay in his hands. If we give Him the broken pieces of our heart and mind, He will put us back together again. For many years I did not give God my pain because I was so ashamed of what had taken place between my uncle and me and all the crazy stuff that I had done because of it. I did not really know the true unconditional love that God had for me, and at the time, I did not know how to release the hurt and receive his unconditional love. I had no one to coach me through that. When the enemy was yelling at me that I was unlovable, God was whispering just how much He really loved me. The truth of God's authentic love had to take root in me in order for me to move forward and trust him with my pain and with my delivery.

Even though I had forgiven, the hurt was still imprinted on my soul and there were times when the enemy would bring back to mind all the pain of abandonment, rejection, and abuse that I had suffered. This was his attempt to capture my mind and take me back to a place where I would easily fall back into agreement with the anguish that I had released. To be honest, there were days that he was successful. There were days when I wanted to say "the heck with forgiveness, I was done wrong, taken advantage of and misused and they should pay," but mercy and grace reminded me that if I do not forgive, then I will not be forgiven and that my pain was not wasted but it has a purpose. I was encouraged by Holy Spirit to continue on with the process.

Forgiveness and healing is a process and they cannot be rushed. The process requires a series of actions that lead to a result and in this case that result would be wholeness. For those of us who have been wounded repeatedly, there are layers upon layers of negativity concerning ourselves and the people who committed the trespasses. This negativity weighs heavily on us and smothers who we really are. Our true identity of who Christ has made us to be is stifled. We relentlessly struggle with our thoughts as we are constantly challenged with changing our mindset to accept the fact that we are indeed free from the bondage of the trespass.

The enemy does not want us to be free. He wants us to continue to live a life of depression, hopelessness, and condemnation because when we yield to these emotions we begin to waver in our thoughts and actions, resulting in emotional and mental instability. We once again entangle ourselves in the very thing that we have been set free from. Satan knows if he can place the yoke of bondage upon us then we will be unable to reach our destiny in God. But because Messiah has died for us, we are resurrected in Him and through this powerful blessing we have been made free and are new creatures in Him, having the old things (our past) pass away (2 Corinthians 5:17 KJV). With Christ we experience newness and are released from the things that held us captive to our past. We no longer have to associate ourselves with the old man and everything that happened to him. We are free! Glory to His name!!!

There were several things that I had to do in order to receive and maintain my deliverance and freedom. Notice that I said, "I had to do." In order to be free, we have to fight for freedom. Remember, we are engaged in a spiritual war and it is against an unseen enemy who is relentlessly battling for our souls. We cannot physically fight Satan, put him in jail or tie him up; it would be nice if we could, but we can't. We must engage in spiritual combat.

The enemy is not just going to let us go. Even though we receive Christ as our Savior, the enemy fights tenaciously to keep a foothold in our lives. He has enjoyed wreaking havoc in our lives for so long that he gets angry when we decide to surrender all and go God's way. He is in a constant war with God for our minds, will, and emotions and he is treacherous. Let me put it to you like this: when a pimp has a prostitute who has been bringing in good money to him, he does everything in his power to manipulate and control her so she will stay with him. When she decides that this is no longer what she wants to do with her life and leaves, the pimp does not let her go easily. He uses several tactics to get her to stay. He tries to convince her that she needs him and that she will not be able to make it without him. He may go as far as physically abusing her to instill fear. If she is a drug addict, he constantly supplies her with her fix. He tells her that she will never be more than what she is now and there is no hope for her because she is worthless.

Most prostitutes have been abused at some point in their lives and they have already been broken. The Council for Prostitution Alternatives, Portland, Oregon Annual Report in 1991 stated that: 85% of prostitute/clients reported history of sexual abuse in childhood; 70% reported incest." So to a mind that is already shattered and emotions that are already damaged, the pimp uses these tactics to manipulate and play on her weaknesses. If she is not careful, she will begin to look at her current situation and agree with the lies of the pimp and lose her conviction to leave. In order for her to move on, she has to be strong in her conviction of getting out. Even though the pimp is trying to plant that seed of discouragement and exploit her weaknesses, she has to press forward and move past all that he is saying. She has to get to a place where she recognizes her life is at stake and that she is worth more than what the pimp is telling her. Sometimes she has to leave everything behind and literally run for her life.

It is the same with us. When we decide to leave the anguish of the past behind, the enemy uses all types of tactics to prevent us from moving on. He uses unforgiveness because he knows without it we walk in bitterness and are spiritually blocked from fully receiving from God. He tells us that God will never forgive us and we might as well give up. He tries to convince us that the pain and suffering is all that we'll ever have and it's who we are. He tries to instill fear to paralyze us so that we are unable to walk in the victory promised to us by God, and he exploits our weaknesses to try to cause defeat. But if we are sure in our conviction for being delivered and set free, we can rise above the voice of the devil and hear the voice of the Lord who is saying, "*Come unto me, all ye that labor and are heavy laden, and I will give you rest* (Matthew 11:28 KJV)," and begin to run for our lives. We have to see victory even if it's not manifested in front of us. If we see it, we can fervently move toward it leaving our past behind.

Philippians 3:14 reminds us, "*Brethren, I count not myself to have apprehended: but this one thing I do, forgetting those things which are behind, and reaching forth unto those things which are before. I press toward the mark for the prize of the high calling of God in Christ Jesus.*"

We are admonished to leave behind those things that hold us down and hold us back so that we can move forward into the abundant life that God intended for us to have. Satan is a thief and his job is to steal, kill, and destroy the abundant life promised by God; but Christ has come so that we can live a rich and full life, a life free from condemnation, shame, and rejection. When we allow Satan to control us through our hurt, we place ourselves in a position to live low. He knows that life in Christ will cause us to live on a higher plane because of Christ's overflowing forgiveness, love, and guidance. Once we come into the full understanding of the freedom we have in Christ and in forgiveness, we relinquish that poverty level of thinking.

I knew that in order for me to be free I had to participate in my own deliverance. There were some things that I had to do in order for me to be loosed from the grip of the enemy. The only way that I was going to be successful in achieving my breakthrough was to partner with God. In this partnering, God showed me some things that I had to walk in.

Accept God's Salvation and Love:

God's love for you and me goes beyond human comprehension. We will never, I believe, fully understand the depths of his commitment to and love for us. His love is unconditional, unrestricted, absolute, and pure. His love is without boundaries and is full of compassion. It reaches down to the deepest pits and pulls us out of the grips of destruction. God's love establishes us and places us on a sure foundation in him. His love is matchless and unquenchable. Nothing compares to it and nothing can ever replace it. The Father's love conquers all things and through his love all things are made new. The Word of God tells us that He loved us so much that He gave his only begotten son so that we might not perish but have eternal life (John 3:16

KJV). God sacrificed himself in order that we may be free. There is no love greater than the love of God.

I had received the gift of Salvation while I was in Bermuda. I knew that I needed God in my life but after I received him, I did not know how to let him reign in my life. I did not know the depths of his love for me so I equated his love to that of man's love. In order for me to allow God to heal me, I had to come to a place where I could allow him to love me. I had to trust him and believe that He was not like every other man. He was not going to use me and cast me aside. I did not have to wonder if I had to jump through hoops to keep him; no, Jesus is in a class all by himself and his love comes from a genuine and untainted place. His love extends from the heart of the Father. Once I accepted that God truly loved me, I was able to trust him and see myself through his eyes and not through the eyes of the abuse. I was no longer that tattered little girl who had experienced love only through the selfish gratification of others. When I stopped seeing myself through the eyes of the abuse, I was able to allow God into the secret places of my mind and emotions that I had kept hidden from him. In doing that, I released myself into his hands for healing, deliverance, and breakthrough.

Come to Terms with What Happened:

I had to stop being angry about what happened and stop asking God why it happened and accept that it did happen. Also, as shameful as it was for me, I had to own up to the part that I played in the incestuous relationship. Although it started off as molestation of a ten-year-old child, it evolved, over time, into a consenting affair, as much as one of that age could consent. My consent was my willingness to keep it a secret and indulge in the act. I had to release the denial and own up to the truth of how I contributed to that ungodly relationship and as appalled and disgusted as I was with it, I had to own it. When I came to terms with it, I was able to repent of the sin and receive the pardon that I needed. By doing this, the enemy could no longer use that sin against me. My confession and repentance revoked the legal access that he had to my emotions. The door of immorality had been shut and sealed with the Blood of Christ. I had confessed my mess, told God all about it and allowed the Blood of Jesus to eradicate it.

Be Honest with God, Repent and Receive Healing:

There came a time when I had to admit how very angry I was with God. Of course, one would never dare say that they are mad with God because that is something that we just don't do. We don't question God, and we definitely do not openly express our disappointment with God, at least that is what we have been taught. Well, He already knows. God knows everything about us. He is a good Father and He makes it His business to know everything that concerns us. Psalm 139 lets me know that God knows my thoughts before I think them and He knows every word that will come forth from my mouth before I speak them. So our anger, depression, and every emotional state that we may find ourselves in are no surprise to him. It took a while for me to admit how angry I was to myself as well as to him. There were times when I was deep in depression and I would ask hum, "Why did You let this happen to me? Where were You when all of this was taking place?" For a while I remained distant from God because I did not understand how He could allow such an injustice to come upon a child. I went through the motions of going to church and putting on a good show for the people, but the anger that I had toward him prevented me from receiving any type of real healing and intimacy that I so needed from him. When I did not get the answer that I wanted from him, I adorned the mask that suppressed everything.

When we are honest with God about how we feel about the situation, He is able to meet us at that place of anger. He understands that you are mad and He is not mad at you for being mad. He understands that that is a reaction to the pain that you are experiencing. He knows that if you allow him, He will give you beauty for your ashes and use that painful experience in your life to pull someone out of his or her depths of anguish. God does not waste pain and He will use your pain to breathe life into someone else who has been suffocated by the coils of despair.

Once I was honest with God and became spiritual naked before him, He was able to come in and speak to me through teachings, sermons, and quiet time. I know now that the pain was not in vain. I no longer blame God, but I thank Him for allowing me to go through and to come out victorious.

Break Covenant (Agreement) with Abuse:

A covenant is a binding agreement. When one is abused one comes into covenant or agreement with all of the issues that are birthed from the abuse. Unknowingly our soul comes into agreement with low self-esteem, bitterness, unforgiveness, anger, the feeling of worthlessness, and so much more. Once the healing process begins, you no longer find the need to associate yourself with the issues that were birthed from the trespass. Your identity is no longer wrapped up in what the abuse depicted you to be and you begin to walk in the identity that God has given you in him. You verbally break covenant with those spirits that kept you bound. As your healing progresses, you will see yourself no longer agreeing with the things that enslaved you but coming into agreement with all God says that you are.

Prayer: *Father God, I thank You for being my deliverer and my healer. I thank You that I no longer have to walk in condemnation and guilt caused by the abuse that I endured in my life. Your Word states that I am a new creature in Christ and old things have been passed away and all things have been made new. I thank You for the newness and for delivering my soul from the past. I repent for walking in covenant with the things that kept me bound. Right now I break covenant and come out of agreement with low self-esteem, fear, anger, control, bitterness, unforgiveness, and a feeling of* *worthlessness. I come into agreement with love, joy, peace, forbearance, kindness, goodness, faithfulness, gentleness, and self-control, in Jesus' name.*

Breaking Soul Ties:

In order to walk in deliverance, I had to break the ungodly soul tie that was birthed through the incestuous relationship I had with my uncle. This soul tie kept me emotionally bound to him and if I was going to have any success at having a healthy relationship with myself and a marital relationship, I had to cut the spiritual umbilical cord that kept me spiritually connected to him. In order for me to break the soul tie, I had to repent for participating in the act. Once I received my forgiveness I was in a position where I could renounce the spiritual connection.

***Prayer**: Father, I come before you in the name of Jesus, I repent for participating in the sin of fornication, adultery, and incest with _____. It was against Your will for my life and I seek your forgiveness. I now renounce myself from the ungodly soul tie formed between myself and _____ and I break these ungodly soul ties in Jesus' name.*

***Prayer:** Father, I come before you in the name of Jesus, I forgive _____ for molesting me. I thank You that You are able to release me from the shame, hurt, and guilt that were formed through this ungodly act. I now renounce myself from the ungodly soul tie formed between myself and _____* *through the ungodly sinful act of molestation. I break these soul ties in Jesus' name.*

Take Down Strongholds:

"For the weapons of our warfare are not carnal, but mighty through God to the pulling down of strong holds" (2 Corinthians 10:4 KJV). Strongholds are a pattern of faulty thinking that the enemy uses to control how we act, react, and respond in a manner that is outside the will of God. We can pull down these strongholds by continually feeding our mind the Word of God. The Word of God is the only weapon that is effective enough to defeat the weapons of the enemy, *"The word of God is quick, and powerful, and sharper than any two-edged sword, piercing even to the dividing asunder of soul and spirit, and of the joints and marrow, and is a discerner of the thoughts and intents of the heart"* (Hebrews 4:12 KJV).

Cast Down Imaginations:

"Casting down imaginations, and every high thing that exalteth itself against the knowledge of God, and bringing into captivity every thought to the obedience of Christ" (2 Corinthians 10:5 KJV). Imagination is a powerful thing. Our imagination gives us the ability to think or create what is not real in our mind. The enemy uses our imagination to get us to form a negative image of ourselves. This image is nothing but a lie that he uses to deter us from the truth of who God says we are. In order for us to cast

down these images and to bring our thoughts into captivity to the obedience of Christ, we first must know what God perceives as right. Any thoughts or actions that goes against the teachings and character of Christ must be seized and destroyed. This is the only assurance we have of maintaining our victory. We must repent of those thoughts that lead us to faithlessness; we then must recapture those thoughts and replace them with words of faith confession and with the Word of God.

Change Your Mindset by the Renewing of Your Mind:

"And be not conformed to the world: but be ye transformed by the renewing of your mind, that ye may prove what is that good, and acceptable, and perfect, will of God" (Romans 12:2 KJV). God's will for us is to be whole. We are admonished in the scripture to be not conformed to the way the world thinks. We are to resist being molded into the thinking, conduct, and value system of the world. Satan is the god of this present day world and we are not to be blinded by his tactics (2 Corinthians 4:4 KJV). He wants us to think that we are defeated and hopeless and if we conform to this pattern of thinking we will live a life of defeat and hopelessness.

We renew our mind with the Word of God. As we inject the Word daily into us, we are tearing down the strongholds of the enemy and replacing them with the strongholds of faith in who God says we are and the promises that He has for us. As the Word of God renews us we will begin to walk in faith, power, and peace. Jesus tells us in John 8:31-32 that if we continue in the Word, the word will keep us walking in freedom and we will have victory over the lies of Satan; *"If ye continue in my word, then are ye my disciples indeed; and ye shall know the truth, and the truth shall make you free."*

Confront Your Abuser:

Facing your abuser is probably one of the hardest things that you may have to do. This meeting will bring closure and the needed release for forgiveness for you and your abuser. I faced my uncle in 2010 and had forgiven him but since then I have dealt with the residue of the abuse. It is not there to the extent as it was, but there is still some residue. When you truly forgive there is no emotional turmoil tugging at your soul. Each time the enemy brought up the offense I decided to forgive.

I contacted my uncle to let him know that I was writing this book. His response was positive because he was proud that I was going to be a published author, even though the subject was not so flattering. When I spoke to him, I assured him that this was not a book of retaliation or exposure. I reiterated that I had forgiven him and myself and I wanted what was best for him. The conversation that we had set me free in areas which I did not realize I was still bound in. There were many things that he shared that gave me insight into what he went through as a child and the things that he had experienced as an adult. For so long I wondered how he got away with doing what he did to me when in fact he was not getting away at all.

As we spoke, he revealed to me the things that he endured in his life before and after the molestation and incest took place. He described some things that transpired in his childhood and I could spiritually see how the enemy captured him as a child through the things that he was exposed to. He shared with me the things that had transpired in his adulthood. He disclosed to me that he has encountered victims of sexual abuse and how that brought him to the realization of how the incident must have affected me. He stated that what took place was what he regretted most in his life and if he could take it back he would. He apologized and because I had a heart to receive, I could hear the genuine expression of regret in his voice, which allowed for final release. The Lord opened up the door for ministering to take place and I was able to share the goodness of the Lord with him. We have never really had an uncle and niece relationship and will probably never have that type of bond. However, I can truly say that it is the development a friendship. Before forgiveness, I could only see him as a sexual predator, but now, Christ has given me the heart and the eyes to see him as a soul who needs salvation in Christ.

Staying in the Presence of God:

In order for us to stay victorious, we have to stay in the presence of the Almighty God. Remember, Satan is the spiritual pimp that wants to exploit our weaknesses for his own gratification. Now that we are free, we are responsible for walking in freedom. Galatians 5:1 states, *"Stand fast therefore in the liberty wherewith Christ hath made us free, and be not entangled again with the yoke of bondage."* We have been set free and we need not walk hand in hand with the things that enslaved us. We stay free by knowing who we are in God through the Word, communicating with God in prayer, and keeping a watch on what we receive through our eye, ear, and mouth gates. If we stay in the presence of God we are able to submit to Him. This submission gives us the power to resist the enemy when he tries to implant lies in us. When we submit to God and resist the enemy he will flee, James 4:7.

Walking into victory is a process so do not be hard on yourself if you do not see immediate results. Remember, you have carried the hurt and shame for so long that it has become a part of you and you have learned to function in it. However, you must choose daily to walk in deliverance. Some days may be harder than others because the devil will come and remind you of the hurt and pain. You have the authority through Christ Jesus to stand against the enemy and to walk in healing. Let the Word of God wash your mind and be mindful of your thoughts.

The reality of the abuse will never go away. It happened and it was a terrible trespass, but you are no longer a victim of that trespass for you have overcome.

CHAPTER 11

Chosen

Sexual abuse is an unspoken topic in our churches today but it seems that it is steadily on the rise. Every Sunday we sit next to men and women who are mentally and emotionally locked in a cell due to childhood sexual abuse. My story is just one of many.

When God gave me the vision for this book over two years ago, I was very reluctant to write it. That "hush don't tell" spirit came and encouraged me to shut my mouth. I did not want people to know the things that I had done and I did not want to revisit the memories. Shame began to speak to me and I did not want people to look at me differently or change their opinion about me. I knew that this coming out would have a very negative affect on my family and the last thing I wanted was to cause hurt and pain to those that I love the most. Clearly I was missing the bigger picture. God, in his grace, told me that my testimony was not to embarrass me or to put me on the spot, but to reach someone who was struggling with the aftermath of this crime.

I have often wondered why God chose me to go through such a trial as this. I came to realize that from the beginning of time, I had been chosen to endure so that I could be a conduit of God's healing and delivering power.

"Before I formed thee in the belly I knew thee; and before thou camest forth out of the womb I sanctified thee, and I ordained thee a prophet unto the nations" (Jeremiah 1:5 KJV).

In this passage of scripture, God was encouraging Jeremiah. God had ordained Jeremiah a prophet before he was born, a mouthpiece to carry the Word of God to his people. He knew the trials that Jeremiah would face but He also knew that He would be with Jeremiah and that his trials, as harsh as they were, would not overtake and destroy him. It is the same with us. God knew us before we were conceived and He knows all that we will go through. He gives us strength to endure and to achieve the purpose that He has set out for us to achieve. He guarantees in his Word that no weapon that is formed against us shall prosper (Isaiah 54:17 KJV). The weapon that the enemy used against you and me was the trespass of sexual abuse but his attempt will not overcome us because we will rise and proclaim the healing power of Jesus Christ.

As unfair as it may seem, you and I went through so much so that we could be an encouragement to someone who does not have the courage or the skills to be healed. God trusts us with this assignment and with this mission and He is with us every step of the way.

God has given to us His beauty for our ashes; He will cause us to relinquish fear and rise above the shame of our youth, and he shall give us double for our trouble.

"To appoint unto them that mourn in Zion, to give unto them beauty for ashes, the oil of joy for mourning, the garment of praise for the spirit of heaviness; that they might be called trees of righteousness, the planting of the LORD to glorify Him." (Isaiah 61:3 KJV)

"Fear not; for thou shalt not be ashamed; neither be though confounded; for thou shalt not be put to shame; for thou shalt forget the shame of thy youth, and shalt not remember the reproach of thy widowhood anymore." (Isaiah 54:4 KJV)

"For your shame ye shall have double; and for confusion they shall rejoice in their portion; therefore in their land they shall possess the double: everlasting joy shall be unto them." (Isaiah 61:7 KJV)

This is your time to ARISE and be healed and take back everything that the enemy has stolen from you.

Peace and Blessings

CHAPTER 12
Prayers, Declarations and Confessions

Prayers of Salvation:

Heavenly Father, I come to You now, I acknowledge You as God, creator of Heaven and Earth. Heavenly Father I confess that I am a sinner.

I have sinned against You. I believe in my heart that Jesus Christ is Your Son and You sent Your Son to Earth, and that he was born of a virgin. I believe that Jesus Christ is the One true sacrifice for my sins. I believe that Jesus Christ was crucified on a cross as a sacrifice for the sins of the world, sins that have blinded me and separated me from You. I believe, Heavenly Father that You sent Jesus Christ to personally die for me. I believe Jesus Christ, Your Son, took upon Himself all of my sins and the sins of all mankind. I believe Jesus, who knew no sin, became sin for me that I may receive Eternal Life.

I believe You raised Jesus Christ from the dead and He is alive and well, seated at Your Right Hand in Heaven. I now repent (turn) from my sins and choose to follow and obey Jesus Christ as my Lord and Savior. I ask You Jesus Christ to be the Lord of my life and to lead me in all areas of my life. Jesus Christ I receive You as my Lord and Savior with all my heart and believe that You are my King and my God. Lord Jesus Christ, fill me with Your Holy Spirit, and use my life as a willing vessel. Heavenly Father, I ask that my life glorify You. Thank You Heavenly

Father for my salvation by fain in Jesus Christ and the Truth of Your Word, in Jesus' Name. Amen.

For those who cannot say that prayer try saying this prayer first: *Heavenly Father, I come to You and ask You in Jesus' Name to set me free from any wrong thoughts, fear, doubt, unbelief, believing any lies, any lies of the enemy the devil, or demonic spirits, any thoughts that I have that are hindering me now in coming to You. I ask You, Father God, to deliver me now of all hindrances to becoming Your born-again Kingdom child, in Jesus Christ's Holy Name. I resist the devil and all his demonic spirits must flee and leave my presence. Lord God, remove the lies and the hindrances and help me so I can say the above prayer of salvation in earnest from my heart. I ask You to force out, drive out, and bind all evil things far away from men, Jesus' Name. Amen.*

Prayer To Release Strongholds:

Strongman called Spirit of Bondage, *I bind you in the Name of Jesus Christ along with all of your works, roots, fruits tentacles links and spirits that are in my life. I cast you out of me along with all of your works, roots fruits, tentacles, links and spirits and I loose you from me and I force you unto out darkness in the Name of Jesus Christ. I ask You, Heavenly Father, to loose into me Liberty and the Spirit of Adoption according to Roman 8:15.*

Strongman called Spirit of Fear, *I bind you in the Name of Jesus Christ and declare that all of your works, roots, fruits, tentacles, links and spirits are dead work in my life in the Name of Jesus Christ, and I bind you and I loose you to go wherever Jesus Christ sends you and command you not to come back into my presence again. I ask You, Heavenly Father, to loose into me the Power, Love and A Sound Mind according to 2 Timothy 1:7*

Strongman called Spirit of Heaviness, *I bind you in the Name of Jesus Christ along with all of your works, roots, fruits tentacles links and spirits of broken heartedness, self-pity, rejection, depression, inner hurts, despair, abandonment, loneliness and suppressed emotions that are in my life. I cast you out of me along with all of your works, roots fruits, tentacles, links and spirits and I loose you from me and I force you unto out darkness in the Name of Jesus Christ never to come into my presence again. I ask You, Heavenly Father, to loose into me the Comforter, Garment of Praise, The Oil of Joy according to John 15:26 Liberty and the Spirit of Adoption according to Roman 8:15 and Isaiah 61:3.*

Strongman called Perverse Spirit, *I bind you in the Name of Jesus Christ along with all of your works, roots, fruits, tentacles, links and spirits of child abuse, incest, rape, molestation, sex perversions, lust, pornography, Incubus/Secubus, homosexuality, lesbianism, and masturbation, I bind you in the Name of Jesus Christ and declare your works dead in my life. I loose you from me and I* *loose you to go wherever Jesus Christ sends you and command you not to come back into my presence again. I ask You, Heavenly Father, to loose into me Your Spirit of Pureness and Holiness according to Zechariah 12:10 and Hebrews 10:29. Amen*

Prayer for Releasing Bitterness*, Heavenly Father, I come to You now in the Name of my Lord and Savior Christ Jesus. Heavenly Father, life seems so unjust, so unfair, the pain of rejection is almost more than I can bear. My past relationships have ended in strife, anger, rejection, resentment and bitterness.*

Father, help me to let go of all bitterness and resentment. You are the One who binds up and heals the broken-hearted. I receive Your anointing that breaks and destroys every yoke of bondage. I receive emotional healing by faith according to Your Word, Isaiah 53:5 "and with His stripes we are healed." I thank you for giving me the grace to stand firm until the process is complete.

Thank You for my wise counselor, I acknowledge the Holy Spirit as my wonderful Counselor! Thank You for helping me work out my salvation with fear and trembling, for it is You, Father, Who works in me to will and to act according to your good purpose.

Prayer for Freedom:

Heavenly Father, I come to You in the Name of Jesus. I worship You, for You are the only true living

King. I come to You with thanksgiving and praise in humility, in fear and in trembling. I am grateful for Your love and for the precious Blood of Your Son, Jesus Christ.

Father, in the Name of Jesus Christ, I ask You to expose and bring into light, negative inner vows and strongholds that contradict Your Word and Will. By the breath of Your Spirit, release Your truth as a sword to expose falsehood, curses of self-rejection, self-hatred, and reactive hatred and bitterness towards others. I take up the sword of Your Word and cut myself free from the bondage of generational strongholds and ungodly character defects. In the Name of Jesus Christ, I renounce all relationships dishonoring to the Lord, Heavenly Father, break the power of soul ties over my mind and emotions for myself and for those people.

I proclaim my freedom to be the child of Yahweh God, to live as You intended me to live, filled and overflowing with the light and power of Your Holy Spirit, filled with the life and love of Jesus Christ. I claim the full protection of the shed Blood of Jesus Christ, the Son of the living God over my life for You are a shield about me, my glory and the lifter of my head (Psalm 3:3 KJV). In Jesus Christ's Sweet Name, I pray. Amen.

Declarations:

Words are powerful. God created the world with his spoken Word. What world are we creating for ourselves by the words that we speak? Proverbs 18:21 states, *"Death and life are in the power of the tongue; and they that love it shall eat the fruit thereof."* What are you declaring in your life today – is it life or is it death? Today I challenge you to declare LIFE!!

I Declare -

I am: God's child for I am born again of the incorruptible seed of the word of God. 1 Peter 1:23

I am: Forgiven of all my sins and washed in the Blood. Hebrews 9:14

I am: A new creature in Christ and no longer bond to the old man and old nature. 2 Corinthians 5:17

I am: The temple of Holy Ghost. 1 Corinthians 6:19

I am: Righteous and holy. Ephesians 4:24

I am: Firmly rooted, built up, established in my faith and overflowing with thanksgiving. Colossians 2:7

I am: Chosen and dearly loved by God. Ephesians 1:4

I am: Being changed into His image. Philippians 1:6

I am: Called of God. 2 Timothy 1:9

I am: The light of the world and my light shines bright. Matthew 5:14

I am: The salt of the earth and my flavor is rich. Matthew 5:13

I am: Christ's friend. John 15:15

Confession - I Am What God Says I Am:

Because God so loved this world He gave his only begotten Son, Jesus the Christ. In Him I am all that He has predestined me to be. For according to Romans 8:30 He has predestined me from the beginning of this world. I am accepted in the Beloved and a joint heir with Christ. I am chosen and dearly loved by Christ and the apple of my Father's eye. I am of a Chosen Race, a Royal Priesthood, a Holy Nation, and a people for God's own possession to proclaim the excellence of Him. I am established, anointed and sealed by God in Christ. I am built upon the foundation of the apostles and prophets, Jesus Christ Himself being the chief corner stone.

I am fearfully and wonderfully made and the spirit of low self-esteem has no dominion in my life. I am alive in Christ and I am Holy and without blame before Him in Love. I am strong in the Lord for

Ephesians 6:10 tells me that I am to be strong in the Lord and in the power of his might. And in his strength I am made whole. In his strength I am made the head and not the tail, and I live above and not beneath. For I am more than a conqueror through Christ Jesus who strengthens me. I am righteous and holy and a temple of God, His Spirit dwells in me. I am God's workmanship created in Christ Jesus for good works. I am a daughter of God therefore a daughter of light. And as a daughter of God an enemy to the Devil. A weapon of mass destruction that God uses to take down the kingdom of darkness.

I Peter 2:5 declares, that I am one of God's lively stones and I am being brought up as a spiritual house. I do not have the spirit of fear because I can do all things through Christ because I have received power; power of the Holy Spirit, power to lay hands on the sick and see them recover, power to cast out demons, power over all the power of the enemy. According to 1John 4:4 I shall overcome because greater is He (Christ Jesus) who is in me then he who is in the world. Behold, old things are passed away so I press toward the mark of a higher calling of God to achieve that He has purposed me to achieve. I have the favor or God and grace and mercy shall follow me all the days of my life. I am blessed and everything and everyone attached to me is blessed.

Notes:

Introduction:

Merriam-Webster Online Dictionary,
http://www.merriam-webster.com/ (accessed
November 2, 2013)

Chapter 6 - Spiritual Doors

Win Worley. Host of Hell Series. "Evil Spirits of
Arrested Development, Accessed June 15, 2013
https://www.youtube.com/watch?v=F1PoS-
SgcRA, Taken from Pastor Worley's Host of Hell
Series).

James Strong. The Strong's Exhaustive Concordance
of the Bible (Grand Rapids: Zondervan, 2001),
1518

Chapter 7 – The Tattered Little Girl

Claudia Black. "Understanding the Pain of
Abandonment." Psychology Today June 04, 2010.
Accessed May 30, 2016.

https://www.psychologytoday.com/blog/the-many-
   faces-addiction/201006/understanding-the-pain-
   abandonment

Chapter 8 - What's Hurting Me?

John Coblentz. Beauty for Ashes Biblical Help for the
Sexually Abused (Christine Light Publications, 1999),
   4-11

Chapter 10 – Recovery (The Process of Healing)

Readings on Prostitution. Accessed May 29, 2016.
   30http://www.soc.iastate.edu/sapp/Prostituition.
   pdf

Cindy Trimm. Commanding Your Morning: Unleash
   the Power of God in Your Life. (Lake Mary:
   Charisma House, 2007) 17-38

Chapter 12 - Prayers, Declarations and Confessions

Christian Word Ministries. Prayers (Lexington, KY)

www.ingramcontent.com/pod-product-compliance
Lightning Source LLC
LaVergne TN
LVHW051127080426
835510LV00018B/2278